Tracy Scrimshaw

DIMBOXES, EPOPTS, AND OTHER QUIDAMS

DIMBOXES, EPOPTS, AND OTHER QUIDAMS

Words to describe life's indescribable people

BY DAVID GRAMBS

ILLUSTRATED
BY SIMON STERN

WORKMAN PUBLISHING, NEW YORK

Published simultaneously in Canada by Saunders of Toronto, Inc.
Art director: Paul Hanson
Book design: Michael Alexander Pici
LIBRARY OF CONGRESS CATALOGING-IN-PUBLICATION DATA
Grambs, David.
Dimboxes, epopts, and other quidams.
Bibliography: p.
Includes index.
1. Epithets. 2. English language—Terms and phrases.
I. Title.
PE1447.G7 1986 428.1 86-40202
ISBN 0-89480-155-4
Workman Publishing Company, Inc.
1 West 39 Street
New York, New York 10018
Manufactured in the United States of America
First printing September 1986
10 9 8 7 6 5 4 3 2 1

CONTENTS

EIGHTEEN

BEAU-NASTIES, BUN-DUSTERS & LOUNGE LIZARDS

135

ONLY MALES:
Womanizers, chauvinists, weaklings and duds

NINETEEN

BALABUSTAS, CACKLE-BROADS & MOUSEBURGERS

141

ONLY FEMALES:
Vixens, bombshells, teasers, crones and castrators

TWENTY

BORBORYGMITES, LEXIPHANESES & MONOGLOTS

147

TALKERS:
Arguers, bull-throwers, literati and pronouncers

Finest
FINGERS

PREFACE

THERE ARE CHOICES IN LIFE, and one of them is what word or words to use in referring to another human being. Take one of your acquaintances who happens to be an infuriating procrastinator. You may call him an incorrigible, inconsiderate, exasperating procrastinator. Or a damned sonofabitch of a foot-dragger. Or a x!*$X of a %!#*¢ bleep.

Then again, you could simply dub the fellow a nanocerebral cunctator.

Profanity has its personal satisfactions, certainly. But so, perhaps, do more literate epithets, particularly when they are 1) succinct, single nouns, 2) genuine English words, 3) so unfamiliar as to be provocative, alarming or at least one-upping, and 4) not likely to be found in your cunctator's friendly desk or college dictionary.

Ancient and unusual words abound in our thicker (and older) dictionaries, far more so than most of us would ever imagine. Like slightly uneasy chaperones, labels are often hovering before their definitions: archaic, obsolete, rare; or sometimes a little proviso in italics that the word is pretty much a passing or humorous coinage. It's as if the dictionaries were cautioning us that these surprising little citizens of the English language are long retired: inactive, creaky and maybe best not called upon.

As a foraging nomenclator (compiler of a word trove or glossary), I've called upon some of these words here, but only on those for people—types of people. You'll find no quaint terms for philosophies, architectural members, flora and fauna, technologies, diseases or foreign dishes in this thingless book. I somehow got it into my head that a collection of unfamiliar but quite genuine English nouns designating human beings, in many if never all of their human varieties, would make an interesting little book—a sort of bestiary of "people words" and, at that, ones that could use having a little dust blown off them. Words do, like dictionaries, get old and dusty with or without those chaperoning labels. But human beings?

The vocabulary of our remarkable language is enormous, and its interesting—odd-looking or droll-sounding—terms (or so-called agent nouns) for types of people alone are numberless. But when you undertake a gleaning project such as this one has been for me, you soon discover that a mighty preponderance of our tongue's forgotten or neglected "colorful" words for behavioral or physical varieties of *Homo sapiens* fall into increasing familiar categories: dolts or simpletons; clumsy, boorish oafs; coarse, slovenly women; vain, preening young coxcombs; bawdy wenches, trollops, jades or mistresses; cowards; grossly fat gluttons; mean misers; loud braggarts; gullible imbeciles; whoremongers or lechers; gossips or blabbermouths; base or scheming scoundrels; lazy louts; noisy revelers or drunks; shrewish scolds; wanton pleasure-seekers; wheedling flatterers; nitpicking pedants...

Those just off the top of my head, motifs suggesting that, in dictionaries, at least, some universal human types are more universal—or synonym-attracting—than others.

For the most part, I was interested in words with meanings more specific than those above. I didn't always find them. But I did find many I had never dreamed existed. Who would guess, for example, that there's a word for a neighbor whose house is on fire? (The word is *Ucalegon.*) But in the pages following you will also notice a few entries that are familiar, not at all alien to your eye and ear. Well, I included a few old friends just because I liked the words or saw them as somehow rounding out the word selection (or type-of-person selection) in the book.

Within the definitions of the more than 500 main-entry words in the book, the reader will encounter a few hundred additional (and, I trust, interesting) "people words." These—similarly rare or unfamiliar categorizing or descriptive nouns for various types of people—appear in italic type and, with all of the main-entry words, will be found in the book's index. Pronunciations have been provided for all main-entry words, and the reader may refer to a pronunciation key on page 181.

I hope readers find the book enjoyable, but I also won't be disappointed if its selected contents send word fanciers scurrying on their own into some of those fatter dictionaries. Any use of this slight volume by persons living or dead for superior, recherché name-calling is unintended and purely coincidental.

Brief as this selective book is, it owes a great debt to many other books and authors: to four indispensable lexicons, the Oxford English Dictionary, the second and third editions of Merriam-Webster's International Dictionary and the Random House Dictionary of the English Language; to Merriam-Webster's Collegiate Thesaurus, Sisson's Word and Expression Locator, Everyman's Thesaurus of English Words and Phrases, March's Thesaurus, Roget's Thesaurus of English Words and Phrases, The Synonym Finder, The American Thesaurus of Slang and Theodore Bernstein's Reverse Dictionary; to numerous special dictionaries, especially Joseph Shipley's Dictionary of Early English, Leo Rosten's "The Joy of Yiddish" and "Hooray for Yiddish!" and the Longman Dictionary of Psychology and Psychiatry; to the great Samuel Johnson, H. L. Mencken and Eric Partridge; and, for their own often invaluable word books, to Josefa Heifetz Byrne, Paul Dickson, Claurène duGran, Willard Espy, Stuart Berg Flexner, Robert Hill, J. N. Hook, Russell Rocke, George Stone Saussy III, Susan Kelz Sperling and Laurence Urdang.

More personally, for their diligent editorial help, I thank Lynn Strong and Mac Havighurst.

ACERSECOMIC
Shear fear.

ONE

DENTILOQUISTS, LEPTORRHINIANS & PITHECOIDS

GETTING PHYSICAL

Odd bodies, certain shapes, noticeable faces, strange looks and all sizes

acersecomic (ak′ər sə kō′mik) One who has never had a haircut, who has never sat in the chair of a *chirotonsor* (barber). A rare being, certainly, unless one excepts diehards from the sixties and fresh arrivals from the jungle. But who has not at some point in life been made to feel like an acersecomic by a hair-resenting parent, teacher or sergeant—or corporate boss with thinning hair? For long but clean hair, the acersecomic should know a good *tractatrix* (female shampooer).

aerophagist (âr of′ə jist) The neurotic or somewhat hysterical gaper who swallows or gulps in air at times of stress. What is the sound of an aerophagist? It is the sound of a marathoner just yanked out of an icy river. No mere hyperventilator, this is an oxygen-sucking panter, an instant heavy-breather, a gasper on automatic. Usually set off by a bad scare or shocking spectacle, or maybe by a spectacular pair of legs.

baffona (bə fō′nə) A woman with a slight mustache. A bit of lip bristle seems to be considered more obtrusive, and hence less desirable, on brunettes than on blondes. Actually, this is an Italian word, one wisely brought to our attention for invaluable use in English by author and *logophile* (word lover) Paul Dickson. Blonde or brunette, while any woman can have a mustache, she is never supposed to sport it.

bandersnatch (ban′dər snach′) A fabulous animal in Lewis Carroll's "Through the Looking-Glass," but also, for our purposes, any extremely strange or grippingly grotesque individual in our human world of oddballs. A bandersnatch is a person singularly, remarkably and unmistakably weird, including the freakish nerd, the goofy doofus and the grody dork.

brockie (brok′ē) Anybody with a dirty face (and a word borrowed truly from the barnyard, where it means a cow with a black-and-white face). Brockies include smudged people working on the undersides of cars, housewives on cleaning day, gardeners on rainy days, and children left to themselves for more than a half-hour.

chamecephalus (kam′ə sef′ə ləs) A person having a flattened skull, or sort of an oblate pate or scalloped sconce: not a receding hairline but a receding head. When angry, some of us tend to threaten to make somebody else a chamecephalus with one leveling swing.

conky (kong′kē) Anybody with a big nose, meaning a prominent proboscis or bulbous beak. Like Jimmy Durante, who was affectionately known as "the Schnozz." The scientific study of noses is called nasology. A nose that is turned up is described as being retroussé, and a pug nose is a simous nose.

cyanope (sī′ə nōp′) A fair-haired, brown-eyed individual. A strange word for such a common human being, but at least useful as a conversation-stopper or eye-stopping noun in one's classified personal ad.

CONKY
Outstanding by a nose.

dentiloquist (den til′ə kwist′) The tight-bite who speaks with closed or nearly closed choppers—literally, through clenched teeth. Does one become a dentiloquist through hereditary family traits? Possibly, though keeping the teeth locked may also be a way to keep a grip on the emotions, or even to keep from biting someone. Dentiloquists include Connecticut debutantes, seething parents, failed ventriloquists, and Clint Eastwood.

dolichocephaloblond (dol′i kə sef′ə lō blond′) A Nordic-looking person or, literally, a long-headed lighthair. Dolichocephaloblonds are found chiefly on ski slopes, California beaches and Swedish film.

fustilugs (fus′tə lugz′) A grossly fat person, especially a frowzy female who has so much flesh to lug about that one speaks not of her poised carriage but of her avoirdupois carting. A walking ham factory (or Armour personnel carrier). "Fustilugs" is a good, getting-down dieting word for major flesh schleppers to hang on the fridge door. What the fustilugs lacks is macritude (leanness).

glaucope (glô′kōp′) A blond-haired and blue-eyed person, otherwise known as the lifeguard type or Lee Remick. Like *cyanope* and a few others in this chapter, a somewhat dated anthropological term but one found in Merriam-Webster's Third International Dictionary. If your irises are violet, like Elizabeth Taylor's, you have ianthine eyes.

grinagog (grin′ə gog′) A perpetual, inescapable grinner, whose toothy rictus is an extreme case of positive outlook or ill-fitting dentures. Everybody has at some point met one of these human Cheshire cats, usually to learn quickly that it's exhausting to the cheek muscles to match them grin for grin. If you merely have a flashing smile, you are not a grinagog.

gubbertush (gub′ər tush′) An absolutely top-jaw individual who has prominent, projecting teeth, or a hang-fang. The man or woman with big, front-balcony choppers doesn't like being called buck-toothed, usually preferring to be considered modestly toothsome or possessed of a slight overbite. Then again, how over is over? The "tush" part of this old dialectal word means tooth, but the exact meaning of "gubber" remains a mystery.

gynandroid (ji nan′droid′) A woman with an imposingly masculine body, if not in the crucial gender particulars or privates sector (though "gynandroid" can also mean hermaphrodite). Here's a female whose voice isn't the only thing that's a bit husky, but she's still all woman—unlike the *androgyne,* who may be male or female (the word is more often applied to males) but seems half-and-half in looks, manner or nature.

hemeralope (hem′ər ə lōp′) A person who has vision difficulties in bright light, or is somewhat day-blind and squinty. Hemeralopes are accordingly nocturnal creatures and in extreme cases may unscrew the refrigerator light bulb, avoid striking matches or wear welder's goggles to bed on starry nights. Everybody feels like a hemeralope now and then, usually the morning after. The counterpart here is the *nyctalope,* who has special visual difficulties in faint light or on dark days. Any person whose vision is less than perfect is an *idiopt.*

killbuck (kil′buk′) A fierce-looking (or torvous) fellow, whose mean mien could not only stop a clock but set it two hours behind. Whether a wilderness wild man or glowering barfly, a nasty customer at first sight—not necessarily ugly, but if looks could kill! Possibly a good mate for a stony-visaged female, or *gorgon.*

Leiotrichan (lī ot′ri kən) One who has smooth, straight hair—if not exactly silken tresses, at least locks that aren't jammed. No curls, kinks or frizzies (as on the head of a ulotrichrous individual). To praise somebody who has nice straight hair, you may commend him or her for being felicitously euthycomic. Meanwhile, hair that is wavy is cymotrichous; that is neatly curled, comatulid; and that is long and manelike, jubate.

leptorrhinian (lep′tə rin′ē ən) Anybody with a long, thin nose, or a nicely lean schnozzle. Cyrano de Bergerac, for instance. An imposing sniffer is thought by some to be a mark of either high birth or reassuring ethnicity. And by some nosy women to be an index of another male endowment; or so men hope, or don't, as the case may be. Pinocchio became a leptorrhinian by lying.

leptosome (lep′tə sōm′) A naturally thin or skinny person, generally sharp-featured with fine-textured hair. Another word for leptosome is *ectomorph.* If neither of these is esoteric enough for you, there's also *hyperontomorph.* We need these spare synonyms, as there are far fewer terms in English for thin people than for fat people. If you don't want to call your girlfriend a lovely leptosome or nubile hyperontomorph, you can get informal and just call her a toothpick, rackabones, beanpole, scarecrow, bag of bones, broomstick or rawbones. A long-legged leptosome is a *spindleshanks* or *long drink of water.*

lungis (lun′jis) The tall, lazy man who is slow about everything, or a shambling, drowsy lout. How could the word be complimentary when it comes from the name (according to some sources) of the Roman soldier who speared Christ? Gary Cooper was not a lungis, but the gawky, overalled, backwoods Neanderthal with the long rifle in the movie "Deliverance" was.

macropod (mak′rə pod′) A person with large feet, or with a pair of shoes not only hard to fill but hard to buy. The most famous anti-macropod song ever written is Fats Waller's "Your Feet's Too Big." The world's largest colony of macropods is called the National Basketball Association. A macropod with truly humongous feet is a *skiapod*—a member of a mythical race who used their feet as sunshades, thereby not cooling their heels.

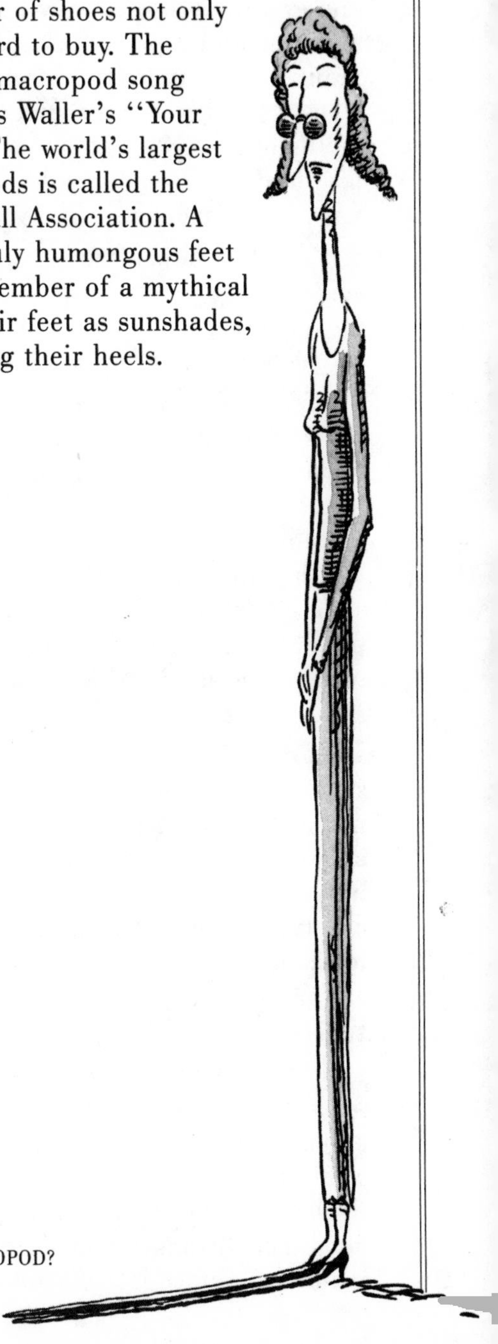

LEPTOSOME OR MACROPOD?
A thin line.

monoculist (mə nok′yə list) A person with only one eye, the other usually having been lost in an accident and replaced by glass. Famous modern monoculists include Sandy Duncan, Sammy Davis, Jr., Peter Falk and Moshe Dayan. The mythological cyclops had one eye, but it was set in his forehead, which made him sort of a literal hairline monoculist.

partan face (pär′tən fās′) A sourpuss, or one who is visibly unhappy and willing to share it facially. Presumably, an over-the-shoulder remark by such a mug-grump would be a partan shot. "Partan" itself is an old Scottish word for crab.

phaeoderm (fē′ə dûrm′) A person whose skin is grayish brown, or ashes-and-cocoa, in contrast to peaches-and-cream, beautiful black or golden tan. Possibly one can become a phaeoderm by sunbathing around heavy smokers or eating too much stale chocolate. If you have misgivings about the possible effect of this word on somebody whose complexion is like a dusty saddle, you might just say he or she is nicely dun-colored.

pilgarlic (pil gär′lik) A bald-headed man, or scalp flasher, and particularly a kind of unfortunate, poor-soul type of baldie at that. The word derives from the similarity of the pilgarlic's glabrous pate to a peeled garlic bulb. You may also describe a hairless head, if you don't want to be too bald about it, as being acomous, depilous or calvous.

pippinface (pip′ən fās′) One of those people who have a smooth, round, reddish phiz (or physiognomy), who are not just apple-cheeked but apple-faced. The pippinface is rubicund, flushed as a blush. A ruddy moonface. An individual with a broad, flat face is a *platyope*.

pithecoid (pith′ə koid) Somebody who resembles a monkey, or a simian simulacrum. That bobbing, long-armed kid down the block who swings wildly on the jungle gym is a definite pithecoid, as is your wiry co-worker with the little nose, button eyes and short, fuzzy haircut.

porknell (pôrk′nel′) A person who is, yes, as fat as a pig, possibly from always wanting to be hogtied to food. As fat as a large pig or a small one? One might answer this by saying a pig is a pig, for the porknell is usually farctate, or stuffed with food. To make matters worse, the word can also mean "some part of the offal of a sheep." (Which part?)

pouter pigeon (pou′tər pij′ən) One of those imposingly erect, matronly and peristeronic (pigeon-like) women having both a sizable bust and a sizable beam—who seem to be coming at you when they're just standing there or, being wide-hipped as well, to be swelling sideways and taking up a whole sidewalk or supermarket aisle. A lady who, bodily, projects heftily.

presbyope (prez′bē ōp′) Or *hyperope.* You probably pass by hundreds if not thousands of presbyopes every week. What is a presbyope? A person who visually is farsighted, who can see things distant better than things near. The ocular counterpart, of course, is the *myope,* or nearsighted viewer. Knowing these two words may cause problems: everybody gets confused enough about the meanings of "farsighted" and "nearsighted."

pyrrhotist (pir′ə tist) A person having red hair, otherwise known as a carrot-top. Pyrrhotists are said to be passionate. A black individual having red hair is known as a *briqué.* A freckly redhead is a lentiginous pyrrhotist. To be just red-haired is to be hirsuto-rufous. To have unusually red hair is to be erythrismal or erythristic.

sinistral (sin′i strəl) A left-handed person, or one who is afflicted with what is very infrequently known as mancinism (as opposed to dexterity, which means right-handedness as well as adroitness). "Sinistral" could well be a word, like "mistral," for a mean wind, and indeed major-league managers look annually for hard-throwing sinistrals to add to the bullpen. Another word for sinistral is *kitthogue.* A person who is clumsy with both hands is ambisinister. A sleight-of-hand artist, or prestidigitator, is a *chirosophist.*

tiqueur (tē ko͝or′) The person who tends to twitch or who has a tic or two, of the facial rather than the insect variety. Twitching is vellication, and one who is twitchy is saccadic. The typical tiqueur, a tic-ing bomb, bursts into winks when nervous or into abrupt, one-shoulder shrugs when thinking. Other tiqueurs play a kind of intermittent one-cheek tango. Whichever, he or she has had a bad shake in life.

whey-face (hwā′fās′) The individual whose complexion is notably pale or like watery milk (if not white as a sheet), as if drained of color. The implication here is thin blood and character weakness: a wan weakling, a pusillanimous paleface.

xanthoderm (zan′thə dûrm′) A yellow-skinned person, or a lutescent (yellowish) individual whose race is Oriental. This is not a euphonious word, but then (not to be too jaundiced) neither are some for people whose hue is black (a *melano* or *melanoderm*), white (a *leucoderm*) or red (the *aithochroi*). Caucasians who have pale skin and dark hair are *melanochroi.*

TWO

LUFTMENSCHES, ULTRACREPIDARIANS & ZETETICS

GETTING MENTAL

Mental whizzes, broad minds, narrow minds, dim bulbs and the self-confused

abderite (ab′də rīt′) Originally, a person from ancient Thrace, a region not noted for its intellectuals. Today, a simpleton or dimwitted yokel, and one with a tendency to scoff at everything. The word sounds like a type of rock, possibly appropriate so far as the skull content of the person is concerned. Let's face it, what we have here is a nanocerebral (stupid) nonentity. A more extreme case, the absolute dumbbell, is an *impos animi.*

acediast (ə sē′dē ast′) A person who is slothful or wickedly lax when it comes to spiritual or religious matters. This creeping secularitis used to be chiefly a monastery disease, but frolicking acediasts are everywhere today. A good place to look is the golf course on a Sunday morning.

analphabet (an al′fə bet′) An illiterate, or one who is literally ignorant of the ABCs. (A person learning the ABCs, or any beginner, is an *abecedarian.*) Analphabets are the unlettered guys in Westerns who slowly and carefully ink a large, wobbly X on the gold-mine deed. Today an analphabet is anybody who cannot read or, worse, would never buy this book. Analphabets make unreliable *epistolarians* (letter writers).

aristarch (ar′is tärk′) A severe but fair critic, as was the ancient Greek grammarian from whose name the word is derived. Society can always benefit from having an Aristarch or two around, if only as a healthy antidote to more easygoing critics, or *logrollers,* who are not above softening their opinions for or trading favors with those whom they consider cronies in their profession. A revered literary personage or arbiter is a *great cham* (a term first applied to Samuel Johnson).

bel esprit (bel′ es prē′) That rare person who has a fine, cultivated mind, social grace and often brilliant wit. A natural at bon mots, repartee, double entendres, badinage and all those other Continental aptitudes. A dinner party's delight, the bel esprit never checks his or her mind at the door.

bibliophage (bib′lē ō fāj′) Or *bibliophagist.* A bookworm or "book eater"; the chronic devourer of pages between hard covers and soft covers, and maybe, in a younger edition, between bed covers (with a flashlight). There are intellectual bibliophages, informational bibliophages and escapist bibliophages, all of whom were born to read and are constantly booked. Bulimic print-mongers are also known variously as *bibliolaters, bibliosophs* and *bibliotrists.*

Boeotian (bē ō′shən) Know anybody who is so incredibly stupid and dull, so unbelievably obtuse, so far from being cultivated, that a word fails you? *Boeotian* (rhymes with "the ocean") is your word, Boeotia having been an ancient Greek land noted for the thickness of its inhabitants' skulls.

ironist (ī′rə nist) The deadly-dry-minded person who loves to be ironic, or is always wryly communicating the opposite of what his or her words say: verbally praising but fundamentally putting down, or expressing enormous interest in a tone of withering indifference or contempt ("I'm *so* impressed"). The ironist has a gift for sustained and restrained mockery, amusing forbearance, tongue-in-cheek enthusiasm. Should be taken literally only at one's risk. The *sicarian* (assassin) of understaters.

latitudinarian (lat′ə to͞o′də nâr′ē ən) A freethinker, unlike the attitudinal hard-liner; one who is broad-minded and liberal regarding beliefs, opinions and, in particular, religious tenets. Today's latitudinarian is either a farsighted ecumenicist or a suspect reformist, depending on the theological latitude.

luftmensch (lo͝oft′mensh′) An airy, impractical dreamer, one of those present but somewhat absent reverie-mavens who walk around with their head in the clouds. Defectively reflective, exotically quixotic, this chronic mind-drifter always seems to be thinking of something or someone else, to be bemused, removed or on cloud ten. Otherwise known as a *reverist* or *musard.*

LUFTMENSCH
Inwardly above it all.

mattoid (mat′oid) Nobody is ever partly pregnant, but what about being semi-insane? If you know an unhinged genius, borderline psychopath, quirky monomaniac, extreme eccentric, deranged philosopher or restless crank, you know a mattoid. The mattoid is not quite around the bend but always has the turn signal switched on. From an Italian word for "insane."

morosoph (môr′ō sof′) A learned or wise fool. Certainly a contradiction in terms, but you get the drift: that type who's royally educated but never anything more than a pedantic jerk and erudite ass, or in worse shape than a backward sophomore. The morosoph is living proof that not all the booklearning or degrees in the world can hide a congenital schnook. A ridiculous pedant is also known as a *lirripoop.*

philalethe (fil′ə lēth′) One who loves to forget, even when it's inconvenient. For the fond disrememberer, life probably hasn't been too terrific, or recent dates and relationships have been disastrous, or guilty reminders are adding up. The philalethe sometimes relies on alcoholic or narcotic fuel to avoid memory lane and reach the state of oblivion. (Could a problem arise in running out of things or people that one longs to forget?) Not to be confused with a *philalethist,* or lover of the truth.

philonoist (fi lon′ō ist) A knowledge seeker, otherwise known as an ideal student or continuing self-educator. This is the instinctive or resolute inquirer and acquirer of facts and ideas old and new, ever on the learn. And, like all ever hungering and well-exercised minds, never a know-it-all.

preterist (pret′ər ist) One who lives in the past, whose greatest pleasures or interests lie in other times and usually other places. No mere nostalgia buff, the unmitigated preterist is the old actress or athlete with the thick scrapbook; the professor who eats, sleeps and drinks Victorian history; the venerable grandparent rocking on the porch, lost in his or her youth. Really devout preterists are *phereters* (keepers of shrines). As a theological term, the word means one who believes that the prophecies of the Apocalypse have been fulfilled.

quick study (kwik′ stud′ē) The fast learner, especially of the lines for a role in a play or of a speech to be memorized. Mentally, a genuine quicker-picker-upper. A swift apprehender who is in a reflective mood would be, of course, a quick study in a brown study.

quietist (kwī′ə tist) A mystically contemplative and passive person, not so much tuned out as tuned above. Preferring a non-mundane approach to life, one that is religious, philosophical, meditative, the quietist is not caught up in the pains of politics or the pleasures of the senses. The quietist is an interior activist.

ultracrepidarian (ul′trə krep′ə dâr′ē ən) One of those presumptuous overreachers who try to address something outside their knowledge or field of expertise and shouldn't, who should know their own limits and don't. A terrible chess player attempting to analyze a grandmaster's game is an ultracrepidarian, as might be a vain and ignorant magazine publisher who decides to have a hand at being a *diaskeuast* (editor). An opinionated unmarried aunt giving honeymoon advice to her niece might also be an ultracrepidarian, and maybe a more fascinating one. The ultracrepidarian is dépaysé: out of his or her element.

witwanton (wit′won′tən) Or *witling.* The would-be wit who tries a little too hard a little too much of the time to be cleverly amusing. The witwanton is always a little off in trying to be always on, straining, showing bad timing or just laying an egg. He or she is pathetically inficete—not witty.

zetetic (zə tet′ik) A skeptical inquirer or investigator, who has doubts, suspicions or misgivings about something but does some further looking into it. The original zetetics were a school of ancient Greek philosophers who were extremely busy naysayers. Today we can still use resident skeptics, people given to taking long, hard looks. An investigator or inquiring searcher is also called an *indagator*, and a thorough surveyor or reviewer of a situation is a *perlustrator*.

THREE

CUNCTATORS, JACK-PUDDINGS & SLUGABEDS

PERSONALITIES

Upbeaters, down-pullers, moody swingers, enjoyers and the seriously unexciting

agelast (a jel′əst) Somebody, anybody, who never but never laughs, with a face that's been deceased for years. Wit? Pratfalls? The latest sick joke? Nothing works with the individual who has a certain perennial air of mirthless coma. The agelast goes through life deadpan. Some agelasts are fearers of gaiety, or *cherophobes.*

ambivert (am′bi vûrt′) Extroverts, introverts—but who speaks up for the ambivert? This is the individual whose personality strikes a nice balance between outgoing sociability and pensive or hesitant self-concern. The ambivert moves comfortably enough in the real, outer world but also has some self-awareness and a capacity for stepping back to ruminate or deliberate.

asthenophobe (as then′ə fōb′) The circumspect stoic, the stiff-upper-lip afraid to admit to weakness of any sort. No self-styled sensitive type who wants to be winsomely vulnerable, the hard-boiled asthenophobe is usually strong on cover-up. Prevalent in the armed services, in board rooms, in street gangs, in age-conscious people, in locker rooms, and in macho husbands and fathers. The ultimate asthenophobe, the person who fears fear itself and will do anything not to show it, is the *phobophobe.*

atelophobe (ə tel′ə fōb′) The driven perfectionist, one with a morbid fear of having things less than numero uno or letter-perfect. Because anything flawed or incomplete reflects on one's imperfect self, of course. The atelophobe has a hangup about perfection and for-the-record neatness, and would rather break than bend.

atrabilarian (at′rə bi lâr′ē ən) A gloomy hypochondriac. If this walking malady doesn't tell you about the long-run illness or latest ache or the recent visit to the *gallipot* (druggist), he or she will let you know about it with a dark and sickly look. Certain sounds announce the presence of an atrabilarian: sniffles, coughs, scuffling steps and deafening muffled sighs. A mere clearing of the throat by a known atrabilarian can clear a whole room. Two other uncommon terms for the dour hypochondriac are *malade imaginaire* and *Argan,* both of which we've borrowed from Molière.

Big-endian (big′en′dē ən) Anybody always making a big fuss about things that are trivial—and a colorful term we've acquired from Jonathan Swift's "Gulliver's Travels." The Big-endian is a Big-deal-er, a worrywart or anal-retentive with a magnifying glass, a major pain over minor matters. And a literary cousin to the *microlipet.*

catagelophobe (cat′ə jel′ə fōb′) The person who is ridiculously sensitive about being ridiculed. Not your laid-back, loose-as-a-goose type of personality, the catagelophobe is given to stiffening, bristling, boiling or collapsing in tears at the slightest hint of adverse criticism, mockery or teasing. Often a thin-skin with a thick ego, or a leptochrous (thin-skinned) peacock.

CATAGELOPHOBE
Paranoid about catty mockery.

crepehanger (krāp′hang′ər) The perennial, down-in-the-mouth kill-joy and depressing, dark presence. The word is derived from that for drapers of black mourning emblems at funerals years ago, dark decorators who worked together with *saulies* or *moirologists* (hired mourners). The crepehanger is a social downer, a breath of fresh gloom. Somebody who looks ahead—and predicts gloom and doom—is a *Cassandra.*

cunctator (kungk′tā tər) A procrastinator, or one for whom there is no time like tomorrow. (And how's this for a word—quite legitimate, if rare—to make somebody do an aural double-take?) For others the cunctator is frustrating, a dilatory lump whose follow-through always dies and whose intentions linger on and on. Anybody who always puts things off soon puts people off. A mere lazy person, or sluggard, is a *lusk.*

curmudgeon (kûr muj′ən) The curmudgeon is cranky, cantankerous and crotchety, an irascibly difficult individual who won't take yes for an answer. Curmudgeons come crustily in all sizes and shapes but usually in old, not in young, and usually in male. About anything, they remain pretty unimpressed. About the world and life, they're more wise to than wise.

cyclothyme (sī′klə thīm′) This is your friend who is so bright and elated at one moment and then, mercurially, so snuffed out and depressed the next. Not an out-and-out (or in-and-out) manic-depressive, but a person with tendencies in that direction. While some people are always on the go, the cyclothyme is always on the up-and-down, a mood-swinger who can be tricky to keep up, or down, with.

enosimaniac (i nos′i mā′nē ak′) "Fear the worst," says the enosimaniac, whose profound concern is always that something really dreadful is going to happen. Not the roast burning but the whole house, or maybe nuclear winter descending right here in Edgevale next week. The enosimaniac makes the simple pessimist a mere dabbler in dread.

ferbissener (fär bis′in ər) A Yiddish word for the sour, embittered person. (The female is a *ferbisseneh.*) Look at that surly scowl, curled lip, condemned-prisoner walk: behold a glowering grouch, a sour puss with a major personal negative philosophy behind it. The only time ferbisseners light up a room is when their clothes are on fire.

flake (flāk) A semi-crazy, the kind of oddball whose approach to things is always unpredictable, usually behaviorally interesting and often amusing. The flake has weird habits, of a public rather than private nature, that may include practical joking or stunts intended to mystify or shock. Or being a pitcher known for conversing with the baseball while standing on the pitcher's mound. A member of the nonpolitical lunatic fringe and, though half nuts, not as deranged as the *mattoid.*

gigman (gig′mən) The respectability maven, and thus, as always with such stolid line-toers, a smug, materialistic, self-righteous philistine. The prestigious car, the big house, the right friends, one's name in the local newspaper—these and other mundanities are the gig of the gigman. Originally, this was a person who owned a gig, or carriage, and whose hat size swelled because of it. Today's self-pedestaling pillar of the community likes to polish the Chrysler. Carriage or Chrysler, a bourgeois is a Babbitt is a gigman.

Heautontimoroumenos (hē ô′ ton tim′ ō-ro͞o′ mə nos) A self-tormenting person—the chronic masochist. Call an agonizer a Heautontimoroumenos and you'll add to the torment and make him or her sufferingly happy. The Heautontimoroumenos (you might as well torment yourself a bit by getting used to saying it) is a sore winner, or a self-made Job who's really into misery. Another old word for masochist is *seeksorrow.*

hypersomniac (hī′pər som′nē ak′) The pillow hugger with a strong addiction to sleeping, who spends so much time recumbent that the only thing he or she makes a dent in is a mattress. A marathon snoozer who can settle down not only for the night but for the day, too. For this it helps to be rich and successfully unemployed.

jack-pudding (jak′po͝od′ing) A jollier or *balatron* (buffoon), and definitely a public one, whose chief purpose seems to be to excite laughter. A 24-hour job, perhaps, but the jack-pudding (who also goes under the name *merry-andrew*) seems to relish the task. For the rest of us, life at the office, the barracks or the disastrously chosen vacation resort can sometimes be hard, and we need every man-jack-pudding we can find to help us keep the laugh lines in shape.

lachrymist (lak′rə mist) The person who cries at the drop of a hat—or at the drop of a wrong word or theater curtain, for that matter. A watery or flebile (tearful or doleful) sort, the lachrymist; a red-eye special. The grim weeper, or the happy weeper, or both. Lachrymists cry for troubled friends, losing ball teams, old movies, beautiful sunsets and happy divorces. And who's to say being a two-hankie personality isn't as worthy as the dry-eyed approach to life? Let the tears fall where they may.

LACHRYMIST
The town crier.

lotus-eater (lō′təs ē′tər) The laid-back hedonist, living a life of idle ease and usually all the comforts, as at a luxury retreat, a tropical estate, or the proverbial desert island on which we all land in our fantasies. Peeling one's own grape becomes an exhausting task for such a languid underachiever. Otherwise called a *voluptuary* or *sybarite.*

malapert (mal′ə pûrt′) A cheeky one, the malapert: saucy, brazen, impudent, but ever lively. An up-front scamp or snip who believes strongly in free speech at any second, even or especially to elders. The malapert has no problem about being forward or taking aback.

naïf (nä ēf′) A naïve person, and often a childlike one. An individual with the gift or the burden of innocence, depending on how one looks at it. Is naïveté caused by foolishness? Excessive inborn virtue? Pure blankness of mind? Whichever, the naïf is that rare human being who remains mystified by or vulnerable to the wiles and guiles of the world. The person who is happy because of being innocent and good is a eumoirous individual.

pococurante (pō′kō ko͞o rän′tā) The incredibly indifferent, careless or nonchalant person, a rolling stone who is less devil-may-care than never-may-care. (The word, from Italian, means "caring little.") The pococurante is gallionic—interested in little, bored with much and fazed by nothing—and might be considered cool if he or she weren't so uninteresting and aimless. Also known as a *Laodicean,* a word derived from an ancient Phrygian city noted for its lukewarm inhabitants. When two pococurantes get together to argue, they have a shrugfest.

prickmedainty (prik′mē dān′tē) A fastidiously finicky or affectedly sweet and good person—and doesn't the word say it all? The prickmedainty is a meticulously and ridiculously precise dresser, a fulsome fashion plate. A prickmedainty is also an insufferably earnest and saccharine person, a real gumdrop goody-goody.

psychasthenic (sī′kas then′ik) A haplessly weak-charactered person, lacking decisiveness and forcefulness and fairly (or unfairly) riddled with self-doubts, anxieties, and little phobias and obsessions. In brief (psychologists are more detailed about these matters), a neurotic weakling, or Woody Allen without the talent.

slow coach (slō′ kōch′) The lentitudinous person, or slowpoke, who takes an interminable amount of time to do anything—move, work, begin, complete or decide. The slowness is not because of interruptions; it's because of a slow-motion temperament that just won't be speeded up. When two slow coaches compete, it's a foot-drag race. The only person who can(not) beat a slow coach is a *laglast.*

slugabed (slug′ə bed′) Or *lie-abed.* The eager-sleeper who flat-out likes to stay late in bed (if not so extreme a dozer as the *hypersomniac*). How many of these reluctant risers are there among us, deaf to alarm clocks and repeated entreaties by already ambulatory relatives or lovers? Lacking euania, or ease of waking up in the morning, the slugabed likes that cozy, early-morning feel of wraparound warmth.

smellfungus (smel′fung′gəs) A grumbling, discontented person, always finding fault with things—the proverbial malcontent and captious critic. The word comes from a grousing character in a book by 18th-century British novelist

Laurence Sterne, who was taking a poke at his contemporary Tobias Smollett for his cranky travel writing. Sterne knew a *kvetch* when he saw one and came up with this nicely pungent epithet. A crabby individual is also known as a *crabstick* or *crotcheteer.*

sobersides (sō′bər sīdz′) The ever serious-minded, solemn person, an earnest Ernest or a grim Grace. A straight-and-narrow type with lips that rarely form a curve and who always manages to look on the heavy side of things. A sedate date or mate for a grave outing.

sophronist (sof′rə nist) The overly, often maddeningly cautious person, a dare-*not*-devil, who likes things to be controlled, regulated. Wary, hesitant, suspicious—and always when action or firm decision is called for. When opportunity leaps forth, the play-it-safe sophronist stands back, antsy about anything chancy. (One thing you need never say to a sophronist is "Take care.")

syntone (sin′tōn′) The go-with-the-flow person, who has an adaptable, socially responsive nature and handles life in a sanely outgoing way. An extrovert, more or less. The syntone doesn't travel with asocial hang-ups or a little bag of neuroses, and seems to fit comfortably into any situation.

tsitser (tsi′tsər) Ever wanted a word for one of those annoying, head-wagging deplorers or hissing commenters always going "Tsk, tsk"? Or "Tsk, tsk, tsk, tsk, tsk!"? From Yiddish (and Leo Rosten) we have the appropriately onomatopoetic tsitser. Like the *doppess,* the tsitser commiserates (tsitsing is a particular style of being a doppess), or offers a kind of black sympathy. But the tsitser also clucks the tongue to judge or scold in a chickenlike way. It doesn't tsit well with most people.

valetudinarian (val′ə to͞o′də nâr′ē ən) Or *aegrotant.* An ailing person preoccupied with sickness or the condition of being an invalid. Here is a mindset that is always under the weather and never over the rainbow. The valetudinarian (a cousin to the *atrabilarian* but not at all to the valedictorian) has a genuine infirmity but has become a chronic patient in life and outlook, usually with those odd habits and ways of the railing ailer; the malady has become a melody.

worrywart (wûr′ē wôrt′) The chronic worrier, with a personality that makes the uncertainties of the future the miseries of the present. "But what if"... "I'm just afraid that..."—this is to be hexed with being vexed. It's hard to reassure the worrywart, who not only is a pessimist but is always looking for evidence. Will a worrywart ever run out of things to worry about? Not to worry.

yenta (yen′tə) The Yiddish name for a woman who is a meddling, vulgar blabbermouth, offering commentary and advice on everybody's business but her own. She has a nose for smoke, an ear for gossip, a mouth for the Smithsonian. The yenta yammers, natters, blathers, jabbers. Definitely not a gift is such gab.

FUSTIGATOR & BÊTE NOIRE
A thwacker and a slacker.

FOUR

FEFNICUTES, GREMIALS & TYPHLOPHILES

FRIENDS AND ENEMIES

Staunch allies, altruists, godsends, hypocrites, liars, schemers, sneaks, betrayers and the cruel

ananias (an′ə nī′əs) A liar, so named after an untruth-teller in the Bible (Acts V) who was reproved by Peter. Ananias, along with his wife, Sapphira, sold a possession in order to contribute the money to the Apostles' common fund but kept part of the money for himself and in effect lied to Peter; both Ananias and Sapphira quickly, as the Scriptures put it, gave up the ghost. Today any liar can be called an ananias, but probably won't give up the ghost for a few years or decades more of healthy prevarication.

ancilla (an sil′ə) The sidekick who helps another to accomplish or master something difficult or complicated. A loyal, trusted aide for whatever task is at hand, from learning Japanese in one month to building a Transylvanian android to just defeating the bad guys. An ancilla can also be called an *adjutory.* A trusted assistant to a magician, incidentally, is a *famulus.*

backfriend (bak′frend′) The false friend, which is to say one's secret enemy; a person who says all the right things and means (for you) all the wrong ones. A tricky-dicky posing as a lovey-dovey. With a backfriend on hand, you never need an enemy. If you'd prefer a more sophisticated synonym for this smiling backstabber, it's *ami de cour.*

bête noire (bet′ nwär′) That particular dreaded or detested or feared person (literally, "black beast") to be at all costs avoided, to whom one is perversely averse. An old rival? An aggravating pest? An ex-husband? Whichever, your bugbear and pet hate as a human or subhuman being.

birddog (bûrd′dôg′) A stealer of another person's date; the flirting raider, who moves in and acquires more than just a piece of the action. Usually it is males who are called birddogs. (Should a female who seduces away a girlfriend's date be called a dogbird?) Today's birddog may be tomorrow's home wrecker.

BOODLERS
Two for the money.

boodler (bōō′dlər) The opportunist who gladly takes bribes; for that matter, also the one who gladly offers them. A bribe-groom, you might say. This is your timeless, classic, corrupt public servant, happily augmenting his or her income through under-the-table thievery. The boodler is a hard pocket-liner, too accommodating to financial temptation ever to be a graft-dodger.

cheese-eater (chēz′ē′tər) A rat, or in human terms a rat-fink: a betrayer, cheat, informer or stool pigeon, the scoundrel with the morals of a whiskered alley rodent. Not to be confused with a *turophile*: a genuine and innocent lover of cheese. An eater of bread and cheese (originally as a form of the Christian sacrament) is an *artotyrite*.

compurgator (kom′pər gā′tər) A technical-sounding word for a true friend at court (unlike the *ami de cour*). This is the loyal acquaintance who vouches for the character of another who has been accused of something. The compurgator offers more than empty words, since he or she has to express respect and praise with one hand on the Bible. A swearer of false oaths? A *philoepiorcian*.

dastard (das′tərd) One of those active, sneaky cowards—the kind who do things furtively and maliciously, all the while slyly protecting themselves. Like causing harm to worthier people rather than confronting or competing with them openly. The dastard is the spineless perpetrator, schemer, betrayer; the artist of the cheap shot or worse (like terrorism).

delator (də lā′tər) An accuser or contributor to the accusations against another, or an informer who provides damning information. The delator is often a spy of sorts, the kind who orchestrates surprise downfalls. He or she remains in the background, a whistle-blower of the dirty variety.

Egeria (i jir′ē ə) A trusted female adviser or companion-in-arms (originally, a woman who acted as patroness to a man in public life). The Egeria of mythology was a nymph or goddess who counseled one of the kings of Rome; an Egeria today is a wise and valued "sister" to a woman or man. A guardian, protector or mentor of either sex is a *creancer* or *fanger.*

eleemosynar (el′ə mos′ə nər) Anybody who shows or dispenses tangible charity, from the wealthy philanthropist to the welfare worker to the pedestrian who is generous with handouts. (A person who distributes alms to the poor is an *almoner.*) The eleemosynar is a Good Samaritan, otherwise known as a *charitarian.*

Ephesian (i fē′zhən) A congenial, convivial, typically jovial crony; a boon companion. A friend to share a bottle with, a good-time pal when hair gets let down and heels get kicked up. Truly a jolly good fellow. Also known as a *bon enfant.*

expromissor (eks′prə mis′ər) Not a person who has backed out of a pledge but quite the opposite: one who assumes responsibility for another's debts. Greater love, or money, hath no man. The expromissor not only picks up the tab, he or she picks up one's old unpaid tabs. Thus a marriage proposal might conceivably go: "Will you be my promised?" "Yes, if you'll be my expromissor." This could confuse a fellow.

fefnicute (fef′nə ky$\bar{o}\bar{o}$t′) A hypocrite or sneak. You couldn't make up a better word (it's an old British dialectal appellation) for one of those people who admit what they don't mean or who mean what they don't admit.

foumart (fo͞o′märt′) Or *foulmart.* Somebody who is despicable, whom one is slightly not at all fond of. A simple meaning, and thus a word with helpfully wide application—and an expressive but clean word that begins with a satisfying *f* is always good to keep in reserve for superior name-calling. Not surprisingly, the foumart is also the European polecat.

fustigator (fus′ti gā′tər) A literal clubman—one who has been inspired to beat another or others with a club, stick or Louisville Slugger. Revolutions and riots always seem to bring out fustigators who are quick with a cudgel. In violent times there may be so many pummeling, head-bashing fustigators around that, well, you couldn't beat them off with a stick. Somebody who carries a handy stave but doesn't necessarily use it is a *claviger,* which can also mean somebody who carries a key or set of keys.

gremial (grē′mē əl) A true, bosom friend, to be warmly appreciated and counted on through thick and thin. From the Latin for "bosom" or "lap," gremial also means a member in good standing of a university or society. A staunch comrade is also called a *fidus Achates.*

infracaninophile (in′frə kə nīn′ə fīl′) A fond fan of the underdog, a flouter (*not* flaunter) of the favorite. The infracaninophile prefers the gutsy contender who is down and out, overmatched or daring the impossible. Possibly a person's allegiance to underdogs grows out of a democratic impulse. The term was coined by writer Christopher Morley.

plunderbund (plun′dər bund′) A chewy collective word for any business, financial or political group or alliance of interests that is exploiting the public; a big-league confederation of official or civic thieves. (The word could well mean either a gang of Dutch pirates or a fat man's tuxedo sash, which, jointly, don't seem too far off the mark.) Any plunderbunds around in your community or state?

pseudologist (sōō dol′ə jist) Or *pseudologue.* The skillful or systematic liar, able to pile lie upon lie without batting an eye. A major-league prevaricator, a marathon *ananias,* who not only falsifies but embellishes and makes it all believable. Charming sociopaths and playboy husbands are often pseudologists, also known as *mythomaniacs.*

psychagogue (sī′kə gog′) A therapist or counselor who helps another to adopt a particular life's goal, if only to deal with a personal problem or improve the quality of the individual's or patient's life. Originally, a guider of the soul in the afterlife or a necromancer who conjured up the dead. Today's psychagogue can go only so far to help.

smatchet (smach′ət) A small and contemptible person. A vicious, grotesque little man is one kind of smatchet. A disagreeable and unmannerly child is another. Nobody likes an evil runt, a malefic twerp or a nasty brat. Dealing with a large and contemptible person can be more of a problem, of course, particularly if you yourself are a short person, or *hop o' my thumb.*

snollygoster (snol′ē gos′tər) A sharpie, or a shrewd, unscrupulous opportunist. This sounds like a creature from "Alice's Adventures in Wonderland," but Alice might have encountered one sooner in the U.S.A. than in Wonderland. The original snollygoster was either a grand-talking incompetent politician or an unprincipled lawyer. The meaning of the word is broader today, but there are still quite a few political and legal snollygosters around. Snollygosters like to hornswoggle.

spite fencer (spīt′ fen′sər) The neighbor who has become so unneighborly as to build a fence, wall, barbed-wire hedge or concrete bunker to make a statement to you. A medieval custom that spread westward, physically spiting one's neighbor occasionally rears its ugly fence in suburban and rural American communities. For its erector, the principal ingredients in a satisfying spite fence are not so much bricks, wood or brambles as hostility and view obstruction.

tertius gaudens (tûr′shē əs gô′dens) That third party, whether friend or stranger, who positively—negatively—rejoices at seeing two other people quarrel. A savorer of personal strife, a fan of friction, a far from innocent or disinterested bystander. Let the fight go on! The tertius gaudens possesses that form of bitter contentment known as schadenfreude (or epicaricy), or joy in others' sorrow.

third tongue (thûrd′ tung′) A person who slanders, backbites or bad-mouths, and a term from the Bible. The third tongue (or *famacide*) has nothing good to say and has it to say specifically about someone. A tongue that the calumniating owner should bite and never does. Sometimes somebody becomes a third tongue out of resentment at being a second fiddle or a fifth wheel.

transfuge (trans′fyo͞oj′) The deserter of or fugitive from a cause, or one who "fuges" to the other side quicker than tempus can. This is the quick-change turncoat, the begger-off-er, the bailer-outer, the copper-outer who when the going gets rough gets going—to the enemy. A very close relative of the *Vicar of Bray*, and also known as a *tergiversator*, *apostate* or *runagate*.

truepenny (trōō′pen′ē) Nothing less than a solidly honest and trustworthy person. A truepenny, being true-blue, will never give you a wooden nickel, and it's good to know lots of truepennies if you haven't a dime to your name.

tufthunter (tuft′hun′tər) Not a botanist but a sucking-up sycophant or sniffling snob, eager to associate with those who have more class. So called because Oxford and Cambridge students who had titles once wore gold tassels, called tufts, on their caps and attracted—tufthunters. If you can't swat an ambitious phony or toady in the face with a tassel, at least send him or her hunting through the dictionary.

typhlophile (tif′lə fīl′) A helper of the blind. This is a pretty elemental human role, and one for special canines as well. If you're not at heart a typhlophile, you might be a bit short-sighted yourself.

Vicar of Bray (vik′ər əv brā′) Anybody who deserts his faith, beliefs or party, or who definitely has a green thumb for greener grass. The original, 16th-century Vicar of Bray reportedly managed to be twice a Protestant pastor and twice a Catholic cleric. This is not a man of the cloth. This is a man of whole cloth, constantly inconstant.

FIVE

BESTIARIANS, ONIOMANIACS & USUFRUCTUARIES

LIKERS

Enthusiasts, preferrers, cravers and mild maniacs

bestiarian (bes′tē âr′ē ən) Or *philotherian.* The animal lover. The youngster who caretakes every four-legged, winged or coiled species of pet from kindergarten to sweet 16; the picketing animal-rights activist (or *philozoist*); and the older person who prefers the company of the faithful dog or cat to that of any two-legged being. (A female animal trainer, by the way, is a *dompteuse*; a male tamer of beasts is a *dompteur.*) The archenemy of the bestiarian is the *zoosadist,* the person who gets pleasure out of torturing animals. Pet lovers who torture other human beings with a little too much ascription of human feelings to their favorite creatures are *anthropopathites* (as are people who humanize their gods).

bibliotaph (bib′lē ō taf′) You've heard of bibliomaniacs? The bibliotaph not only loves books, he or she is so possessive as to lock them all up or even bury them in a secret place. The traditional literature-squirreler treasured a rare edition, a fine binding. The modern bibliotaph may be more likely to secrete a stolen volume of erotica or a criminally overdue library book. An actual book thief is a *biblioklept,* who steals, of course, from a *bibliopole* (bookseller) or *bouquiniste* (second-hand-book dealer).

heliophile (hē′lē ō fīl′) A sun lover and, when there's a full noon, a happy submitter to its warming and tanning rays. Unlike the ancient heliolaters, who offered up prayers and sacrifices to our nearest star, the contemporary heliophile is content to bask and perspire. Being solisequious (following the sun), heliophiles like to travel south or west and become brown-as-a-berry tanlings. To bask in the sun is to apricate, which makes a heliophile's suntan oil an aprication application.

lapling (lap′ling) A person who is fond of lying back and resting in a woman's lap. Laplings tend to be male and make their needs known mostly at picnics, at parties where there is a shortage of chairs, and in slow-death scenes in movies and operas.

nemophilist (ne mof′ə list) The lover of forests and woods, or of the sylvan world. The nature lover who most likes the unbeaten paths in tracts of trees and the beauties of coppices, groves and dells; and who of necessity must also be a *dendrophile,* or tree lover. A person who likes the rustic or pastoral life is an *arcadian.*

oniomaniac (ō′nē ə mā′nē ak′) The compulsive buyer, or that person you know who can't window-shop without self-control going right in the window. An uncontrollable purchaser is not an ideal spouse unless one is oneself a compulsive *philargyrist* (money lover) with a compulsively large house. Somebody who is desirous or covetous of objects is pleonectic.

philalethist (fil′ə lē′thist) A lover of truth. The person smitten with the cause of verity will have a difficult but never boring life. Philalethists tend

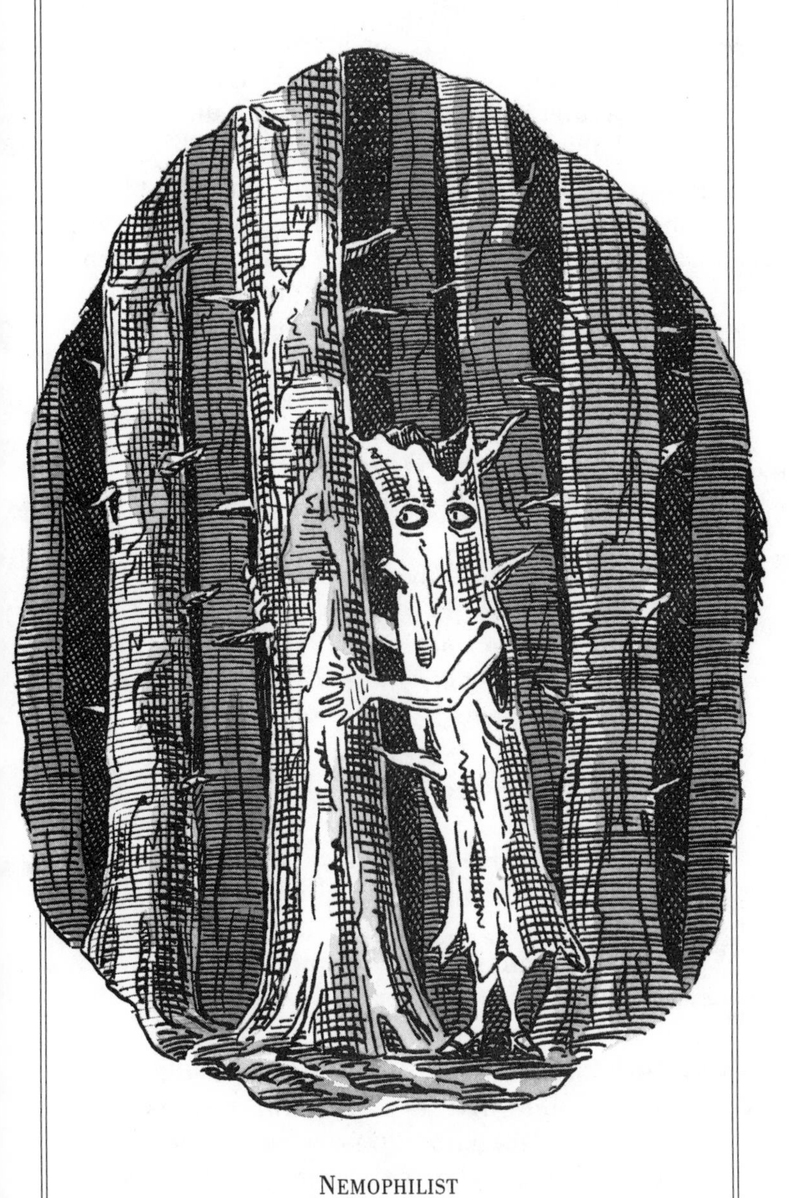

NEMOPHILIST
Preferably, a place in the shade.

to be inquisitive, tenacious, skeptical, clear-eyed and well-informed. They include good, no-nonsense friends, resolute scientists, dogged journalists and suspicious spouses. The person you're always complimenting for having a good bushwa detector? Probably a closet philalethist. Conceivably, a lover of half-truths could be called a semiphilalethist.

philargyrist (fi lär′jə rist) One who loves money, or who is nummamorous or lucripetous. Estimates vary, but there is general agreement that the portion of our planet not covered by water or ice is covered largely by philargyrists. Philargyrists are otherwise known as *mammonists, chrematists, philoplutaries, aphnologists* and *plutolators.* The money lover who is driven by a fear of poverty is a *peniaphobe.*

philocalist (fi lok′ə list) A lover of beauty. There are as many kinds of philocalists as there are kinds of or tastes in beauty. Among them are the *paysagist* (landscape painter), *conchologist* (shell collector), *chakotript* (brass rubber), *bulbul* (composer of sweet songs) and *aulete* (flute player) or *fagottist* (bassoonist).

philocubist (fi lok′yə bist) The aficionado of dice games, whether the battlefield of luck is a casino table in Las Vegas or the bedroom card table at Uncle Joe's apartment. Philocubists also like to let the good times roll on board games if the stakes are right. A major musical about incorrigible philocubists is "Guys and Dolls." A person who throws dice not for fun but to divine the future is an *astragalomancer.*

philocynic (fil′ə sin′ik) A dog lover. The world is pretty much divided into philocynics and ailurophiles, the kitty lovers. A dog keeper, especially someone who looks after greyhounds, is called is a *fewterer.*

philogynist (fi loj′ə nist) Or *gyneolater.* A person who loves women. Perhaps too much is heard of misogynists, and it's good to have a word to remind us that many males (and females) are genuinely and hopelessly fond and admiring of womankind. Not to be confused with the *phylogenist* (expert in species evolution) or *philogamist* (marriage lover).

philopolemist (fil′ə pə lem′ist) The lover of argument, controversy or otherwise verbally mixing it up. A walking combative spirit; a prodder and stickler who loves nothing more than getting the facts down and the hackles up, finding an angle in a wrangle. A philopolemist, sometimes known as an *eristic,* likes to be the center of contention.

physiophilist (fiz′ē of′ə list) The nature lover, whose spirits rise and vital juices flow when released from the mundanities of city life to the beauty of mountains, lakes, forests and seashores. The physiophilist who can no longer fully enjoy the great outdoors without removing all articles of clothing becomes a *gymnosophist,* or nudist.

plebicolist (plē bik′ə list) The individual—politician, above all—who courts the favor of the common people. Sincerity can accomplish this, though astute plebicolists seem more likely to resort to florid rhetoric or phony folksiness. But not all wooers of the hoi polloi are tinhorn demagogues or major dictators. Narcissistic rock musicians, vain athletes, grandiloquent evangelists and schlock novelists can also be plebicolists for sure.

rosarian (rō zâr′ē ən) A person who grows roses. A thorny specialty for the *hortulan* or *horticultor* (gardener), and one not recommended for the *anthophobe* (flower fearer).

toxophilite (tok sof′ə līt′) Or *sagittary.* A lover of the bow and arrow, or the ardent archer. History

UFOLOGIST
In search of a legitimate sighting.

is full of quivering toxophilites, including Robin Hood and his band of bowmen and the renowned archers of Henry V at Agincourt. Archers today mostly hunt or enter competitions.

ufologist (yo͞o fol′ə jist) A devotee of unidentified flying objects, otherwise known as UFOs, and close encounters of an alien kind. Photographs of blurred and hovering flying saucers can be questionable, and it's important for a reputable ufologist to be able to detect a fraudulent snapshot of a piece of lofted dishware. That is, not to be too saucer-eyed. A studier of remarkable creatures such as the Loch Ness Monster and Abominable Snowman is a *crytozoologist.*

usufructuary (yo͞o′zə fruk′cho͞o er′ē) Ever gotten to live in somebody's country house for a summer or to take good care of a friend's Winnebago while she's overseas? Then you've been a usufructuary: an enjoyer of another's property, but with the responsibility of not wrecking it. Having lots of wealthy and generously lending friends makes it easy to be a willing and happy usufructuary.

SIX

BATHYSIDERODROMOPHOBES, MOMES & SILLOGRAPHS

DISLIKERS

Avoiders, fearers, detractors, critics, carpers and skeptics

aeroacrophobe (âr′ō ak′rə fōb′) The fearer of flying. This fear is not due to familiarity with airline food. It is due rather to the terror of being aloft in an open and high-up space when somebody else is handling the driving. The aeroacrophobe (or *aviophobe*) likes to keep his or her feet on the ground, or not more than an automobile tire away from terra firma. This is not the case with the *funambulist* or *schoenabaptist* (tightrope walker).

agonist (ag′ə nist) A struggler; a person who is contending, whether in a mental or spiritual conflict or against an opponent for an athletic prize. When you say "How ya doin'?" to someone and hear back "I'm trying to cope," you're probably face to face with a chronic agonist.

ailurophobe (ī lo͝or′ə fōb′) Or *elurophobe*. The person who can't stand cats. Some ailurophobes are allergic to felines and go into a sniff-and-scratch or sniff-and-sneeze attack. Others just think that adored kitties are creepy, stealthy, humpbacked, four-legged egotists that graze against legs, claw the threads out of you and jump into your mashed potatoes. Ailurophobes are also known as *felinophobes, gatophobes* and *galeophobes.*

anti-sabbatarian (an′tē sab′ə târ′ē ən) One opposed to observing the sabbath as it is traditionally (and was once Puritanically) observed by Christians. With the churchly approach to Sunday come into hard times in recent years, the Sabbatarian may be greatly outnumbered by anti-sabbatarians—golfers, late sleepers and mall shoppers. A cousin to the *acediast.*

anuptaphobe (ə nup′tə fōb′) The male or, especially, female who has a single fear—a fear of remaining single all her life. Even individualists usually want to end up as one of a pair. After 30, anuptaphobia can lead to desperation, possibly to wedding bells with a rush-order spouse.

bathysiderodromophobe (bath′ə sid′ər ə-drom′ə fōb′) Somebody extremely fearful of subways. A general bathysiderodromophobe just doesn't like riding in tunnels beneath cities. (What if the street falls in?) Many bathysiderodromophobes have visited or lived in New York City. The Manhattan variety loves efficient and safe underground public transit but has never known it. Is there light at the end of the tunnel?

clinophobe (klī′nə fōb′) One who is fearful of going to bed. Many clinophobes are probably less than nine years old. Frustrated insomniacs may also dread climbing into the nightly rack, of course; it becomes wake-up time. A person whose real fear is darkness or the night is an *achluophobe, scotophobe, nyctophobe (nictophobe)* or *noctophobe.* Fear of going to bed with somebody else is quite a different matter, one that the *coitophobe* (fearer of sexual intercourse) must cope with.

cnidophobe (nī′də fōb′) The person whose grand terror is of being stung, as by a bee or a wasp. Picnicking or summer-strolling cnidophobes tend to overreact to airborne insects, jumping up at the sound of a distant, droning airplane or swinging wildly at a stray dogwood petal that grazes the cheek. More specifically, one who fears bees in an *apiphobe* or *melissophobe,* and the fearer of wasps is a *spheksophobe.* All cnidophobes have their ears cocked for bombination (buzzing or droning).

cynophobe (sin′ə fōb′) The dog fearer or hater, and not just the mailman and milkman. The avoider of canines knows that their bite is even worse than their bark, not to mention the shedding and drool of certain breeds, the yelping and neuroses of certain other breeds, and the big or small do made on sidewalks by all breeds. To say nothing of the cold sweat induced by the sight of a Doberman or German shepherd or the ineffable odor of a heavily rained-on dog.

embusqué (äm′bo͞o skā′) A nice little bit of French that English has adopted for the person who tries to avoid military service, as by taking a government job or getting a teaching position in academia. A shirker, or a guy who's suddenly and desperately inseparable from civilian life, and who definitely doesn't want to be part of a *tirocinium* (group of raw recruits) but may instead end up a member of a *coffle* (group of chained-together prisoners). During the years of the Vietnam war the embusqué's lot was different from that of the *enragé* (militant radical) and *manifestant* (demonstrator).

Hellenologophobe (he len′ō lō′gə fōb′) One of the hoi polloi who have an antipathy toward esoteric terminology of Grecian etiology. That is,

HELLENOLOGOPHOBE
To hell with Hellas!

a person strongly turned off by Greek-derived scientific (or pseudoscientific) words, or by forbidding Grecisms. The Hellenologophobe will probably not be happy as a technical writer, lexicographer, physician or professor of Western philosophy.

malist (mā′list) A believer that the whole world is evil or bad. Not a wishy-washy form of pessimism, to feel that the entire planet has gone to hell in a handbasket. The malist tries to avoid seeing newspaper headlines and may even get upset at the daily crossword puzzle. Even no news is bad news.

misarchist (mis′är kist) The hater of any kind of government except possibly self-government—that by his or her own self (or *antarchist).* The misarchist is not a cheerful taxpayer, voter or citizen, and generally dislikes any authority that impinges on one's, well, freedom to dislike.

misocapnist (mis′ə kap′nist) Not merely a nonsmoker, but a wincing, hand-waving hater of tobacco smoke, from which he or she gets only a contact low. Where there's smoke (of a butt puffer), there's fire (of a misocapnist's temper). In restaurants and other public places, misocapnists increasingly demand to be separated from the *nicotians,* the cloud-generating customers.

misodoctakleidist (mis′ə dok′tə klī′dist) The piano student who just hates to practice. How many millions of misodoctakleidists have suffered from their key aversions? How many, hard-pedaled by parents into learning the piano, have felt that sitting down to practice octaves and études is like pulling a chair up to a meal of cold dominoes and graph paper? Practice makes perfect, and makes misodoctakleidists, too.

misologist (mi sol′ə jist) The thick-skulled individual who hates any rational discussion or honest argument about an issue—who mightily resists becoming enlightened. Know a few dozen fanatical ignoramuses like this? This is a mentally frigid *collocutor* (engager in conversation) who knows whereof he or she doesn't listen. If you attempt to bounce ideas off a misologist, you may hear them clatter to the floor.

misopedist (mis′ə pē′dist) The hater of children. When the baby is trundled out to coo, the misopedist sees not an infant but a stubby little flesh-colored *homunculus* (grotesque little creature). He or she does not enjoy passing schoolyards, visiting couples who have a brood of brats, or answering the door on Halloween. Is this adult behavior? To paraphrase W. C. Fields: "Anybody who is a misopedist and a *cynophobe* can't be all bad."

misoxene (mī sok′sēn) Or *xenophobe.* The hater or avoider of strangers. By "strangers," the misoxene means not only the door-to-door salesman but unintroduced people at parties, new neighbors, lost souls asking directions. Adopting this philosophy definitely puts you at a social disadvantage. Misoxenes tend to be rural people, and some enjoy sitting in a porch rocking chair and stroking a shotgun.

mome (mōm) Or *momus.* The carping critic, finical faultfinder or petty put-downer. Always on the watch for the flaw or the flub and quick to assail the detail. For some reason, family discussions reveal certain relatives to be momes. A whole troop of momes bearing down on somebody is a cavil-ry. Related to the mome is the *Zoilus,* a hairsplitting pedant or critic; and the *pilpulist,* a Talmudic hairsplitter.

musophobe (myo͞o′zə fōb′) The lady—or gent—terrified of mice. Nobody admits to fearing wee, sleekit, cow'rin, tim'rous beasties (as Robert Burns described them), but it can take only a squeak or nibble in the night to reveal the musophobe. Generally speaking, musophobes not only fear a live mouse but also don't want to get anywhere near a dead one.

pyrrhonist (pir'ə nist) One totally skeptical in his or her philosophy, and hence no mere random doubter of this or that. For the pyrrhonist (also known as an *acataleptic* or *didymist*), there is no trusting even what one feels or perceives; life is an iffy cabaret in which there is no such thing as certainty. Keep on shrugging and send in the clowns.

sillograph (sil'ə graf') Or *sillographer.* Not just a satirical person but one who writes satires or (a *pasquilant)* lampoons, or who has a penchant for literary mockery. You'll find sillographs in the pages of humor magazines and in the wings at "Saturday Night Live."

spermophobe (spûr'mə fōb') The fanatical avoider of (surprise!) germs; also known as a *bacillophobe* or *bacteriophobe.* (The morbid fearer of sperm—*or* of loss of sperm—is the *spermatophobe.*) Crazy about soap and wincingly wary about drinking out of the same glass or sharing an elevator with a sniffler, to say nothing about backing down onto a strange toilet seat. One famous spermophobe was Howard Hughes, who in his final years avoided all contact with potential germ carriers. The hyperhygienic germ commando doesn't trust doorknobs—you never know where they've been—and brushes after each meal and cataglottism (soul kiss). Are all spermophobes squeaky-clean themselves?

theomicrist (thē om'ə krist) A belittler of God. (One who merely resists God or the divine will is a *theomachist.*) Much is heard of atheists, agnostics and blasphemers, but what of theomicrists? The Almighty complainer tends to speak up when the world is having a particularly bad year. The blame goes right to the Top.

tomophobe (tō′mə fōb′) One who dreads or resists any kind of surgery—who possibly would accept any consequences rather than go under the knife. The tomophobe may have started out as a fearer of pointed objects (the *aichmophobe*) or as somebody who hates needles (the *belonephobe*). Or he or she may have nothing against bodily incisions per se but a lot against doctors and surgeons, whom they might consider *hippiaters* (horse doctors).

SEVEN

AMBIDEXTERS, FACTOTUMS & PEDOTROPHISTS

LEADERS, EXPERTS, PARAGONS AND TALENTS

People with skills, brains, confidence, determination, imagination or good luck

ambidexter (am′bi dek′stər) One who uses both hands with equal capability and ease—who can sew, swing a golf club or beat a mean egg lefty (as *sinistrals* do) as well as righty (as *dexters* do) or vice versa. In the sport of baseball, the bat-wielding ambidexter, or switch hitter, literally swings both ways. A related human creature is the *dextrosinistral,* who is naturally lefty but learns to write righty.

amicus humani generis (ə mē′kəs hōō mä′-nē jen′ə rəs) A philanthropist, or "friend of the human race," which is the fundamental meaning of this noble calling. You don't have to be rich to be a day-to-day amicus humani generis, but it sure helps.

anax andron (an′aks an′dron) A leader of men or, if you will, a take-charge guy (over a *caudatory,* or follower). An appropriately masculine but euphonious term, it comes from Homer, who applied it to Agamemnon and who certainly wrote at length about men and men's men. General George Patton was definitely an anax andron, and maybe your father, brother, husband, son or boss is, too. Somebody who is not exactly a leader but is a good master of ceremonies is a *symposiarch.*

aristologist (ar′i stol′ə jist) A true artist when it comes to the hows, whats and whos of dining that involves quite a few guests—as in the case of preparing a grand banquet. A culinary aristocrat from soup to nuts, knowledgeable in all that goes into making a repast a fine one in substance, service, company and atmosphere. Aristologists are big wheels on meals, cooks or restaurateurs who know their courses, and their rules. As a 19th-century writer, quoted in the Oxford English Dictionary, put it: "The Romans . . . defied all the rules of aristology by their abominable excesses."

autoangelist (ô′tō an′jə list) One who does his or her own communicating, whose messages come personally—not through a friend, representative, personal secretary or general runner-of-interference. This is the individualist who doesn't duck responsibility or pass the buck to another person when it comes to breaking bad news or to reporting an embarrassing failure—somebody perhaps to be admired in the modern world of intermediaries and spokespersons. Royal *nuncios* or *internuncios* (messengers) of older times who were fated to be the unlucky bearers of bad tidings (and to be punished for them) must have had a single thought: "If only my king were an autoangelist." Or, if only they, the luckless messengers, had *succedanea* (substitutes) to fill in for them.

autodidact (ô′tō dī′dakt) The person who is self-taught, whatever the skill, knowledge or challenge in question. This is the admirable self-starter—and finisher. A functioning, follow-

AUTODIDACT
"Never mind, I'll do it myself!"

through individualist, the autodidact picks it up, book or technique, without having to have supportive tutors or rooters.

beau sabreur (bō′ sä bro͝or′) Or "handsome swordsman": the dashing, gallant adventurer, larger than conventional life and an appealing mixture of fearlessness, humor and devil-may-care panache. A man's man, and certainly a woman's, too. The beau sabreur is an Errol Flynn, a swashbuckling hero. (If he can jump from one horse to another, he's a *desultor.)* A male who is a mere handsome society fellow, or dandy, without a sword, is a *beau garçon.* A swordsman or bravo who is not particularly virtuous is a *spadassin.*

Briareus (brī âr′ē əs) What's happening? Ask the Briareus, who seems to be in touch with or on top of everything. (The word comes from the name of a mythological giant who had fifty heads and a hundred arms.) Not the crack switchboard operator, but the lightning-minded dynamo who is up on this and on that and on him and on her. As the French might put it, au fait and au courant, the best at being abreast.

cher maître (sher mā′trə) The admired master in an artistic profession, especially in painting, and one often addressed by this title. A teacher either directly or indirectly, the cher maître is looked up to by pupils and *epigones* (artistic followers or imitators) as a model of knowledge and skill, if not as a genius. Age is no barrier: if you're brilliant enough, you can be a cher maître at 30.

coryphaeus (kôr′ə fē′əs) A leader of a school of thought, religious movement, or political party or group. (Originally, the leader of the chorus in a Greek drama.) The coryphaeus is the individual with both a cause and a following; and, usually, with duende (charisma). Not to be confused with a *coryphee,* a dancer or chorus girl.

Croesus (krē′səs) An enormously rich person (as rich as Croesus, the Lydian king of the sixth century B.C.). This is the fellow who never has to ask the price, because he *can* afford it, always. Being a Croesus saves one from having to bargain-shop, marry into money and watch "Dynasty" with material envy. Another name for a Croesus is Rockefeller (any one of them).

débrouillard (dā′brōō yär′) The ever capable and self-reliant person, independent, competent and resourceful. An autonomous ace, the débrouillard is the ideal contractee, executive, helpmate, or anybody else who doesn't have the time or need for a supportive supporting cast. A solid soloist who cuts it alone.

dimbox (dim′boks′) The smoother-over of disputes, an expert at getting others to make up (and not at all to be confused with a dim bulb). If you need an *irenicist*—a calming influence, a human peace pipe, somebody neutral to help bury your hatchet—here's your third party. Newspapers today never seem to want to refer to veteran mediators and expert negotiators as capable dimboxes.

factotum (fak tō′təm) Or *bricoleur.* The ace handyman, that useful person who can do all kinds of work or who smoothly handles different responsibilities. This includes the jack-of-all-trades around the house and the jill-of-all-trades around the office—not the sensitive concentrator who has to focus, thank you, on one and only one thing at a time. The factotum personally takes care of, delegates or organizes, even when chewing gum.

imaginator (i maj′ə nā′tər) The person who not only imagines but also creates something in the process, such as a work of art or of the intellect. The imaginator taps his or her personal vision or singular mind to originate, devise or express. With far too many proclaimed but doubtful "creative geniuses" in the world, it might be nice to get back to this word. Man as maker or creator is *homo faber.*

mensch (mensh) The wonderfully solid, decent human being, thoroughly honorable and compassionate. In the mensch (a Yiddish word) these are warm, not cold virtues: this man or woman, as the case may be, gives off fellow-feeling. More loosely, a real mensch is a real pal, for being generously helpful or understanding in a particular situation. Short-term or long-term, this is a trustable *tellurian,* or earthy earth-dweller.

mnemonist (nē′mə nist) A skilled memorizer and adept at methods of not forgetting—a memory freak not of the nostalgic variety. Good mnemonists (or *mnemotechnists*) become actors, spies, presidential interpreters, journalists or interviewers, loyal friends who will "cover" for somebody—or heads of how-to-improve-your-memory schools. Zip codes, telephone codes and words spelled like this one have increased the need for astute memorizers.

neoteric (nē′ə ter′ik) The modern or contemporary person, having new thoughts, outlooks or approaches; especially a modern writer, an author marked by newness if not by greatness. (One blindly unaware of change or new ideas is a *dodo.*) A rare word for the newfangled modernist (or post-modernist), and also for somebody who is into new words and phrases, or neoterisms. The person who likes to invent, or coin, new expressions is a *neologist.*

nonesuch (nun′such′) A person without equal or rival, the model, paragon or class act who attracts nothing but superlative plaudits and comparative envy. The nonesuch (as opposed to the non-entity) reminds us that though all are created equal, some go on creating or exemplifying unequally and become—well, Michelangelo. Also known as a *nonpareil* or a *nulli secundus.*

optimate (op′ti mət) A patrician or, for our modern democratic purposes, one of the best or the brightest, sweetly élite. Optimates attend the best schools, get the best salaries and travel to the best places. Nations are sometimes governed by optimates. And sometimes, as in a kakistocracy (or government by the worst), by lowlifes.

pedotrophist (pi dot′rə fist) The wise parent who knows how to raise children. A gift, certainly, particularly to the hip mom-and-dad's fortunate children. (More admirable, perhaps, is the single-parent pedotrophist, who has it together when it comes to carrots and sticks.) Some parents read too many child-rearing books and try a little too hard to be pedotrophists, as their children's analysts can later report.

polyhistor (pol′ē his′tôr) One who is remarkably learned or scholarly in many subjects, and also known as a *polymath.* A rich and mature mind beyond the realm of the mere straight-A student or academic specialist, the polyhistor is a walking Britannica—who is often given a chair by a university. On the other hand, there is the dull, unimaginative pedant, the *dryasdust.*

serendipitist (ser′ən dip′ə tist) The lucky finder of desirable or valuable things or encounterer of wonderful, unexpected experiences that are like wishes come true. For the serendipitist, happenstance is happy and fortuity is felicitous. He or she has a gift for coming upon, turning up, running into and lucking out; and, romantically, maybe for "meeting cute" (as they say about boys and girls in the movies). Do any joys beat the unanticipated ones? Be content, serendipitists, and encounter your blessings.

EIGHT

ANDABATES, GOBEMOUCHES & SCHLIMAZLS

FOLLOWERS, FALTERERS AND LOSERS

People who are submissive, hapless, clumsy or dupable

Alphonse and Gaston (al′fonz ən gas′tən) Two people who trip over each other being polite ("You go first." "No, after *you*!") so that the situation gets nowhere. Put two painfully courteous people in the same room and you'll have such deferential standoffs—over eating the last hors d'oeuvre on the plate, picking up the check or passing through a doorway. From characters created by American cartoonist Frederick B. Opper.

âme damnée (äm′ däm nā′) A slavish follower or dupe of another and thus a "lost soul"—lost mostly because of the person being followed. Whether a benighted, mindless member of a religious cult or an otherwise intelligent person at the service of an evil millionaire, the âme damnée has taken a wrong turn and become a victim astray or a tragic *peccadillant* (sinner).

andabate (an′də bāt′) One who is hoodwinked, in the dark or virtually blind to the realities of a situation. An interesting term that first referred to a type of gladiator who was required to fight blind, in a helmet having no eyeholes (certainly an activity less pleasant than being blindfolded and thwacking open a Mexican party piñata). The andabate is a person not in the know, struggling but hopelessly benighted.

anorchus (an ôr′kəs) Physically speaking, one who has no testicles. Figuratively (or disfiguratively?), a person who lacks what these male appurtenances signify: courage, backbone, guts.

asinus ad lyram (a sē′nəs ad lī′ram) The "ass at the lyre," or someone who tries his hand at something creative, like singing or composing a speech, without possessing the necessary talent. An eager klutz or an unfortunately activated philistine. Possibly a *daubster*, or bungling painter. Sort of an artistic bull in a china shop, an embarrassment to himself and his audience—except possibly on the old "Gong Show."

autologophagist (ô′tō lō gof′ə jist) The eater of his or her own words. Autologophagy is the fate of those individuals who are foolishly and explicitly sure of themselves and turn out to be resoundingly wrong; who are force-fed back their own opinion, boast or prediction that was ill-advised.

autophobe (ô′tə fōb′) The socializer who does not like to be alone, stuck with his or her own company. Not one who relishes privacy and needs to be solitary now and then, the autophobe tends to be a desperately gregarious joiner and may even feel lonely in a bathroom without a mirror. Also known as an *eremophobe* (or *eremiophobe*) or a *monophobe,* and a counterpart to the happily asocial *solitudinarian.*

bibliobibuli (bib′lē ō bib′yə lē) Those who read too much, and hence tend to be unaware of or oblivious to the real world. Bibliobibuli, then, are bookworms with blinders, or print porers, delvers and scanners who don't believe a word of what they're not reading or that a truck is coming until they see it in print.

AUTOPHOBE
Unfazed by a chilly reception.

blinkard (bling′kərd) The individual who is always blinking and, what's more, whose moment-to-moment eyelid closings betoken a definite lack of intelligence or perception. The blinkard looks uncomprehending and, by cracky, is. A person who blinks only one eye and does it quickly and intentionally is a *nictitater,* or winker.

bovarist (bō′vər ist) The one who has a tragically unreal, romanticized self-concept, as does the daydreaming title character of Flaubert's "Madame Bovary." Rather than merely harboring delusions or fantasies from time to time, the bovarist walks around inside a would-be-me notion—the great adventurer, the brilliant actress, the appreciated writer. A good role, but in a production playing to a house of one.

cockshy (kok′shī′) A person made the object of attack or the butt of ridicule (and a word from an old English game in which sticks were thrown at a rooster). If you're a cockshy, you've become a sitting duck, a tempting target, a convenient scapegoat or just a sad laughingstock.

commorient (kə môr′ē ənt) One of several or many who meet their death in the same calamity, or one who (the word means "dying together") perishes at the same time somebody else does. Romantic hotheads who make blood pacts are sometimes sort of vowing to be commorients.

criticaster (krit′i kas′tər) A critic by profession—but no more than an inferior, petty reviewer. (A petty anonymous writer is an *anonymuncule.)* For every respected critic, there are four or five second-raters abroad. To become a criticaster you don't have to have a lack of discernment, an eagerness to divulge obvious ideas and cheap opinions, and sources for free theater or film tickets or books, but it helps.

FUTILITARIAN
Borne on fancies of flight.

futilitarian (fyo͞o til′ə târ′ē ən) The hapless type always engaged in futile ventures or pursuits—fame before the age of 21, get-rich-quick schemes, harnessing solar energy from the moon. But the quixotic Ralph Kramdens with grandiose notions keep at it, never quite making it. The right stick-to-itiveness, the wrong goals, methods or talents.

gerascophobe (jə ras′kə fōb′) The age-conscious type, with a constant dread of growing—or looking—old. This kind of worry can age a person. Celebrities who visit plastic surgeons and have faces that gleam like greased pie plates are often gerascophobes (or *gerontophobes*). Youngsters who gag about getting real old, like 30, are not. The blessing of naturally remaining youthful in looks despite one's age is called agerasia.

gobemouche (gôb mo͞osh′) The "fly swallower," or that unfortunate person who will believe just about anything. Give this Gullible Gus, or *rube*, a bit of rumor or a lot of cock-and-bull, and he'll run with it. Another rare word for a born dupe is *gudgeon*.

laglast (lag′last′) Back there, bringing up the rear far from the front-runner, this is the one who dawdles, shuffles, hangs back to the last; or (if you like words beginning with the letter *l*) the laggard, the lazer, the lingerer, the loiterer, the lumberer, the last-placer. Last place is vitally important to the laglast.

looby (lo͞o′bē) A fellow who is large, lazy and awkward, or sort of a non-incredible hulk. When disliked, the looby is a clumsy oaf; when liked, he's a big lug. Unlike the supple-jointed *limberham* (a term also applied to a toady, or someone too supple behaviorally), loobies don't make good *tripudists*, or dancers.

martext (mär′tekst′) A blundering preacher, or a clergy member who performs a bad service by not being on top of things when it comes to reading holy text or prayers, or who sort of blows his or her lines before God's flock.

mooncalf (mo͞on′kaf′) A foolish, fickle, moony person (or child of the moon), or one who happens to be both simple- and absent-minded. A dreamy dolt. Then there's the *moonraker,* a not too bright rustic (who would try to rake the moon out of its reflection in water)—or a native of Wiltshire, England.

nebbish (neb′ish) A haplessly, sadly unfortunate and innocuous being, kind of a cross between a poor soul and a sad sack. Along with *schlemiel* and *schlimazl* (and the similar Yiddish words *schlump, zhlub, schnook, schmendrick, schmo, nayfish, yutz . . .*), a jerk. As Leo Rosten explains, the schlemiel trips and knocks down the schlimazl, and the nebbish repairs the schlimazl's glasses.

nose of wax (nōz′ əv waks′) An extremely pliant person, easily influenced, convinced or misled. A dupe or *cat's paw.* If you want to win an argument or feel like the great persuader, you can't do better than to approach a heart-of-gold, feet-of-clay nose of wax. A woman with a shiny nose job is not a nose of wax. She's a *rhinoplast.*

nudnik (nŏŏd′nik) The monumental bore, prodigious pest or awesome nag who always makes his or her presence painfully felt. This nuzzling nuisance specializes in unstellar conversation and unwanted advice and is often too thick-headed and self-involved to take a hint or a powder. When you can't predict what a nudnik will say, you can still predict that it will be a mighty tedium.

pigwidgeon (pig′wij′ən) A kind of immediately forgettable, insignificant, simple person, as nondescript in personality as in appearance. Rarely successful at making an impression, the ever innocuous and faceless pigwidgeon is socially invisible and forever being taken for granted. A pigwidgeon is also called a *squidgereen.*

quidam (kwī′dam) While the special individual or V.I.P. whom you know isn't just anybody, the quidam *is* just anybody: one who is unknown or unnamed, an uncertified certain person. In short, a what's-his-name (or what's-her-name). This makes a person who used to be such an anybody but who is now a definite Somebody a quondam (erstwhile) quidam.

schlemiel (shlə mēl′) The woefully clumsy, foolish, gullible, unlucky—and uncomplaining—jerk. Forever socially maladjusted, the schlemiel is a born loser to be pitied, the one who can't fix things, who gets cheated as a customer, who drops trays of food and is never taken too seriously. Worse, a schlemiel looks like a schlemiel: physically graceless, clearly inept—and totally lacking in sex appeal. A more Anglo-Saxon word for a fumbler or bumbler is *hoddypoll.*

schlimazl (shli mä′zəl) Like the *schlemiel,* a born loser, but to the nth degree. As the Yiddish saying goes, the schlemiel spills the soup, the schlimazl is the one it gets spilled on. When a schlimazl appears, luck runs in the other direction. Or, according to four one-liners strung together by Leo Rosten: when a schlimazl winds a clock, it stops; when he kills a chicken, it walks; when he sells umbrellas, the sun comes out; when he manufactures shrouds, people stop dying.

tatterdemalion (tat′ər də māl′yən) A person wearing shabby, torn clothing or virtual rags. To be a tatterdemalion and retain a sense of dignity and social poise is not easy, but it can be entertaining; we would be sorely deprived without the comedy of Charlie Chaplin and other genteel hoboes (or *stalkos*) in American silent movie comedy. No matter how threadbare, the tatterdemalion is still a notch above the *slubberdegullion,* who is a filthy slobberer and sloven.

NINE

LUCY STONERS, NYMPHOLEPTS & THE UNCO GUID

BELIEVERS, CONVERTERS AND SPOILSPORTS

Dogmatists, proselytizers, zealots, idolators, smug opiners and petty minds

adiaphorist (ad′ē af′ə rist) The person who may or may not be religious or a believer but who has not the slightest interest in points of religious controversy. ("In the end, we all worship the same God.") Latitudinarian or (as one says today) ecumenical, the adiaphorist sees little point in theological quibbles.

agathist (ag′ə thist) The *meliorist,* or forward-looker who believes that the world and things in general are heading for the better. Thus in things that most people regard as evil or tragic, such as virulent diseases, calamitous earthquakes, or wars, the agathist can find some ultimate purpose. The optimist (in the word's purest sense) sees the present as being pretty much for the best; the agathist, less content with the present, nonetheless thinks things are inevitably tending toward good—"though perhaps not," as one dictionary explains, "along the best road."

dry nurse (drī′ nûrs′) The person who busily instructs or assists another when no help is called for. You know, pointing, explaining, suggesting to a needless or repetitive degree? The dry nurse is a *didact* (pushy pedant), or something of an annoying, advising *nudnik* whose unhelpful meddling is called teaching at the wrong time, at the wrong place and at the wrong person.

FELO-DE-SE
A fight to the bitter end.

felo-de-se (fel′ō də sā′) Not just a suicide but a "self-felon" who takes his or her own life through an unlawful, malicious act or through being convincingly self-destructive. Both the rash, suicidal soldier and the human-bomb terrorist are felones-de-se (as the plural goes).

grammaticaster (grə mat′ə kas′tər) The petty, self-styled expert on grammar, usually a niggling, precise type who can stab a bony finger at a dangling participle or split infinitive but lacks a true appreciation of writing in all its richness and varied styles. The rule-conscious pedant who sees prose not as good or bad but as right or wrong.

ipsedixitist (ip′sē dik′si tist) The opiner, or opinionated person, who makes dogmatic statements that are anything but proven facts, or whose assertions are borrowed from an "authority." (A dragged-in authority consulted or cited to clinch an argument is called a *Quinalpus.*) Kind of a continual, know-it-all declarer, the ipsedixitist thinks of discussion in terms of neat, convenient little certainties and quotations. A parrot with an ego problem.

Lucy Stoner (lo͞o′sē stō′nər) A married woman who uses her maiden name (not necessarily "Stoner"). This has nothing to do with incognito signings of motel registers, but rather reflects the view that "Mrs." may not be the highest title a female can aspire to. The original Lucy Stoner was a 19th-century American suffragist.

microlipet (mī′krō lip′ət) The petty, high-strung person who becomes upset or irritated by the smallest things, all exercised over the unexpected or disturbing minor detail. A hypercritical crank who trafficks in trifles and makes mountains out of molehills. Another word for a stickler is *punctilionist.*

nephalist (nef′ə list) A total abstainer from alcohol, and otherwise known as a *teetotaler.* Not all nephalists wear long black dresses and take sledgehammers to cases of hooch. Many know more about the dark side of drinking than the guy wobbling next to you at the bar.

nullibist (nul′ə bist) A disbeliever in any kind of spirit, soul or incorporeal being. All those people who talk of a universe of spirit or psychic forces or oneness everywhere? The nullibist—truly solid in his (or her) existentialism, you might say—won't have any of it. That ghostly, airy-fairy stuff just isn't. Nullibists aren't likely to become *colporteurs,* or peddlers of religious tracts and books.

nympholept (nim′fə lept′) The dreamy idealist: someone with a burning enthusiasm for something that can only remain an unattainable ideal, whether spiritual, political or personal. Starry-eyed or wild-eyed, the nympholept has been bewitched with a passion for the impracticable.

opiniater (ō pin′ē ā′tər) The extremely opinionated person; a vocal dogmatist who is armed with firm yeses and nos and, of course, confident of-courses. The opiniater may have a quick, open mind but is more likely to be an insufferable conclusion-jumper.

orthoepist (ôr thō′ə pist) The superarticulator who knows all about the correct pronunciation of words, or orthoepy. Professional orthoepists provide, among other things, the phonetic spellings next to words in dictionaries to show us how to pronounce them. But we have armchair orthoepists, too, those clean-toothed people who make it a point always to be pronouncedly correct in speech and, of course, to correct others. Nobody upsets an orthoepist more than a slack-mouthed person who speaks slurvian, or slurry English. Curiously, as word-collecting author Paul Dickson has pointed out, lexical orthoepists don't agree as to the preferred pronunciation of this very word: should the stress be on the first syllable rather than the second?

peccatophobe (pi kat′ə fōb′) The person continually worried about committing (or having committed) a sin, which makes life a tricky, step-by-step proposition (with no room for looking back). The peccatophobe has a strong sense of right and wrong, or clean and dirty.

philodox (fil′ə doks′) One who just loves his or her opinions—a lot more than yours, for example. The philodox tends to be dogmatic, argumentative, a bit deaf to reason. A close relative of the *opiniater.*

precisian (pri sizh′ən) A precise word for an overly precise person: the strict observer of rules, forms of conduct, procedures, etc. A punctilious line-toer who is not pleased by approximation or omission. Unlike *heteroclites,* precisians always go by the book.

rectitudinarian (rek′ti to͞od′ə nâr′ē ən) An all-right person in the worst sense: one who continually practices being completely right, quite correct, so proper and often devilishly pious in life, or a self-righteous pain. An upright holier-than-thou-er, the rectitudinarian has little fun, being too occupied with personal sanctimony.

unco guid (ung′kō go͝od′) The community's prim-and-proper puritans, or those who profess religiosity and conduct that is strictly moral. If high-profile goodness and sober-minded living are your thing, the unco guid is your crowd. An old Scottish epithet that deserves more use by all of us less circumspect sinners.

wowser (wou′zər) The oppressively virtuous disapprover of such vices as gambling, shopping on Sunday, dancing and the like—oppressively, because of wowsers' annoying tendency to try to reform non-wowsers. Australia gave us this word for a nagging puritan, though we already had our own version (called *bluenoses*) here. Wowsers have a thing about, not major sins, but petty amusements and naughtinesses that others enjoy. Being antithalian, or opposed to festivity and merriment, they're destined never to have a wow of a time.

TEN

BLATEROONS, ENERGUMENS & SOLIPSISTS

TROUBLEMAKERS

Annoyers, meddlers, intruders, upstarts and bores

agitprop (aj′it prop′) The vociferous, propagandistic agitator or sloganeer, particularly one with Marxist or leftist sympathies such as a rabid *aspheterist* (communist). Not your shy ideologue, the agitprop likes to publicize his or her cause—through a doctrinaire piece of guerrilla theater, a bullhorn, street-corner pamphleteering or some inspirational revolutionary graffiti—and is usually a broad brush for a narrow cause.

ami de cour (ä mē′ də ko͞or′) The fairweather or foul-hearted friend: insincere, definitely not to be trusted. A "friend at court" in French, but that's the slick court of kings and cunning courtiers, not the court of justice, and you wouldn't want your ami de cour to testify on your behalf anywhere. With amis like this, who needs en-amis? A highfalutin synonym for *backfriend.*

anemophobe (an′ə mō fōb′) The thin-skinned shiverer always worried about wind and drafts. ("Is there a window open somewhere?") Recognized by their buttoned-up sweaters and huddled, crossed-arms posture, these chronic draft-evaders can feel a gust in a hothouse or coming around the corner from a whispering Eskimo.

barrator (bar′ə tər) Related to "barrister" only by milieu. Barrators are those constant inciters of lawsuits who would rather have a day in court than a day at the beach. That litigious friend who's always saying, "So I called my lawyer right away..." and "I'll sue her blind!" can be called a barrator or, if you need another word with the same meaning, a *promovent* (a rarer term from the old days of church courts). The barrator might just as well be a *stagiary*, or law student, if not a *leguleian* (lawyer), *Bartolist* (skilled lawyer) or *jurisprude* (showy or pedantic lawyer).

bashi-bazouk (bash′ē bə zo͞ok′) A dangerously out-of-control, undisciplined individual who knows no law; in short, an unmanageable wild man. The word, referring to a one-time group of savage Turks who were military irregulars (indeed), is certainly satisfying to the ear—if dangerous to say to somebody with a violent disposition.

bitter-ender (bit′ər en′dər) The stubborn, sticky holdout who remains inflexible to the end about an issue or disagreement. No giving in, no compromising, no apologizing. The bitter-ender is the philosophical sore loser, who digs in even harder when anybody talks about being reasonable. A bitter-ender who is an unyielding political radical is a *jusqu'auboutist.*

blateroon (blat′ə ro͞on′) Not an old Dutch coin but a constant talker or "blatterer"—at length, a gabber, chatterbox, babbler or prater; or the motormouth, afflicted with the condition known as logorrhea. In short, a *blatherskite.* And a word that nicely suggests a bladder filled with hot air.

blowtop (blō′top′) The male or female who becomes angry very easily or quickly, or a hothead with an especially short fuse. Testy or tetchy. For instance, that friend or relative with whom one always has to avoid certain topics or whose mood must be carefully assessed—and who even then can be unpredictable. This is human fulminating mercury, somebody who hits the red line at a wrong touch. Also known as a *madbrain.*

buttinsky (but in′skē) The continual meddler or interferer in other people's business (or pleasure). The pushy pest who gets a word in not just edgewise but frontally, sideways and from behind. When they're too obnoxious, buttinskies are asked to please become backoffskies.

catamaran (kat′ə mə ran′) A fishwife or quarrelsome scold; that is, a virulent virago, shrill shrew or nasty nag. The word also means a double-hulled sailing vessel, of course, so that the female who overhears you using the word of her will probably think you're praising her sleek lines.

crosspatch (krôs′pach′) A person who is constitutionally ill-natured and disagreeable, who can't decide whether to be a full grump or a mere grouch. Crosspatches like to be peeved most of the time and are peeved if they can't be.

Dogberry (dog′bə rē) Any smug official who is little more than an ignorant, inept busybody or misfunctioning functionary. Dogberrys (the word comes from the name of a bonehead constable in Shakespeare's "Much Ado About Nothing") officiously fuss and bluster and bumble and blunder, all in a day's work.

energumen (en′ər gyo͞o′mən) An individual who is possessed (or seems to be) by demons, who is thoroughly fanatical or single-minded about something—a personal project, a scheme to get revenge, a new approach to life. A diabolical dynamo.

makebate (māk′bāt′) A person with a penchant for stirring up strife between others; a kind of cowardly voyeur or mischief-maker specializing in divisiveness. The makebate likes to see other people mix it up while keeping his or her own hands clean. Otherwise known as a *breedbate* or *boutefeu.*

marplot (mär′plot′) The interferer, well-meaning or not, whose efforts only hinder or ruin a project, plan or endeavor, or whose meddling causes a muddle. The person you wish would "just stay out of it" is probably a marplot—the predictable gummer-up of the works, the intruder whose two cents you don't want. A *buttinsky* who gets (fouled-up) results.

MAUVAIS SUJET
Up to no good.

mauvais sujet (mō vā′ so͞o zhā′) A worthless, disreputable and thoroughly untrustworthy person—in short, a no-good ne'er-do-well or a "bad lot." A reprobate who, like a suspicious-looking customer in a store, should be carefully watched.

pathomimetic (path′ō mi met′ik) A feigner of illness, otherwise known as a *malingerer.* The practicing pathomimetic likes sympathy, attention, warm beds, manipulating other people, getting out of obligations or work, or possibly just the joy of fooling others. A specialist in faked moans, sighs, grimaces, sniffles and limps.

PATHOMIMETIC
Grasping for attention.

polypragmatist (pol′ē prag′mə tist) Or *polypragmist.* A busybody. Calling a busybody a polypragmatist is like calling a conqueror a *debellator* or a gravedigger a *fossarian.* But they are all just that, respectively.

quidnunc (kwid′nungk′) A gossip and newsmonger with, as the word says, a "What now?" personality. The quidnunc cannot keep his or her counsel, preferring to be a practicing purveyor of the latest (or an ambassador of good swill). All ears, quidnuncs never fear the worst about anybody. They hope like hell for it and learn it by heart. Otherwise known as *carrytales* or *talebearers.*

scattergood (skat′ər go͝od′) Not somebody who scatters good around but one who squanders goods. The scattergood is the wasteful person, the wrong-time spender or fritterer-away. A spendthrift, if the stuff being frittered away is money, but also known to be wasteful with possessions, privileges, or gifts from others. Need a word for somebody who depletes funds, exhausts resources or blows a whole wad?

smell-feast (smel′fēst′) The uninvited meal cadger, who can smell out a set table anywhere to get a piece of the edible action. Wherever food makes an appearance, the smell-feast gets a front-row seat. He or she *does* expect a free lunch.

solipsist (sol′əp sist) The self-absorbed, self-referential me-addict, one of those placid, unconscious egoists so involved in their own concerns that they're blind to any other points of view. In philosophy, solipsism is a theory that the self is the only existent thing or the only knowable thing.

But more loosely, solipsists are the not uncommon individuals who place themselves at dead center of the universe, who do not necessarily feel superior but are always self-centered or impenetrably oblivious. For the egotist, the admiration of others is important. For the solipsist, the world is just an extension of the self. Just think of Inspector Clouseau.

stormy petrel (stôr′mē pet′rəl) Trouble is the name of the stormy petrel. This is the uh-oh person whose arrival on the scene usually signals an argument, a fight, a revolution or all-out war. The term comes from the name of a bird believed to be active just before the coming of a storm.

tort-feaser (tôrt′fē′zər) Any individual who has unlawfully wronged another person but without actually committing a crime—just an act of negligence, breach of duty or obligation, libel, or damage. You're surrounded by tort-feasers, or wrongdoers, daily. Know anybody who has trespassed on somebody's property, failed to keep a promise, slandered you, damaged your belongings, stolen your screenplay idea or punched you in the nose? That's a tort-feaser for you. A civil-law term for a major incivility (not involving a contract), but one with a nice ring to it.

ELEVEN

LA-DI-DAS, PERPILOCUTIONISTS & SPANISH ATHLETES

SOPHISTICATES AND WORLDLIES

The charming, the witty, the wily

cosmopolite (koz mop′ə līt′) An urbane citizen of the world, not just a world traveler but a globe-trotter having no particular national attachment—a man (or woman) without a country who is comfortable that way. Cosmopolites thus feel kind of polydemic, or native to several places. Also called *hommes* (or *femmes*) *du monde,* cosmopolites tend to be *polyglots,* or speakers of many languages. They also try not to get oikotropic, or homesick, which in their case could get confusing.

ennuyé (än′wē ā′) A bored person; the citizen of weary dissatisfaction who sings ho-hum instead of hi-ho to life. Ennuyés are not too energized, but then all that yawning, shrugging, and looking for an exit can be somewhat draining. And not only on themselves. A person with a pronounced inability to be attentive to anyone or anybody for any length of time suffers from aprosexia.

Francophone (frang′kə fōn′) One who speaks French fluently, like a native-born Gaul or a sophisticate schooled in Switzerland practically since birth. How many people secretly long to be Francophones, able to burble more than "un peu de français'' at parties, in the bedroom, back at those snooty waiters?

la-di-da (lä′dē dä′) An oh-so-affected person, who is just too-too (or, as the British say, twee) in coming on as genteel, elegant, cultivated or upper-class. A swell who is not at all swell but rather a pretentious put-on.

Latinotaster (la tin′ə tas′tər) The person who has only a sprinkling of Latin but likes to use learned-sounding Latin phrases in conversation or writing. A Classic name-dropper.

perpilocutionist (pûr′pə lō kyo͞o′shə nist) A person who talks through his or her hat, or who doesn't know what he or she is talking about. Perpilocutionists often mean well and just get carried away with their efficient mouths and deficient knowledge. Not to be confused with *dontopedalogists,* who talk with a foot in the mouth.

pseudosoph (so͞o′dō sof′) One who pretends to be blessed with great wisdom. While authentically wise individuals are aware mostly of their own areas of ignorance, the pseudosoph is a poseur who looks to exploit others' areas of ignorance in order to make an impression. Useful here are pensive frowns, knowing looks, robust laughs and avuncular winks.

sarcast (sär′kast′) The one who can never resist being sarcastic, or the constant dropper of verbal sneers—comments like ''Oh, *sure . . .*'' and ''Don't exert yourself too much.'' Your chronic debunker, the sarcast, who can never let something pass without making it fail. Two rival, side-mouthing sarcasts like nothing better than getting together for a good scoff-le.

PERPILOCUTIONIST
All words and no substance.

sciolist (sī′ə list) One who gets the most out of superficial knowledge; a mention-and-escape strategist. Sciolists are everywhere—writing shallow books, calling in to radio talk shows, teaching students in a safe and formulary way, sporting sports statistics and holding forth at saloons. If a little bit of knowledge is a dangerous thing, the sciolist is a dangerous person. A bird of the same feather is the *psilosopher* or *philosophaster,* or superficial philosopher.

solonist (sol′ən ist) A wiseacre, or one who constantly puts on an act about being learned or clever but is a smug little fake—whose wise come-on doesn't come off. Could there be a nicer word for an affecter of wisdom—a smart-ass—than "solonist"? Not to be confused with a *solon* (or *thesmothete*), who is a wise lawgiver.

Spanish athlete (span′ish ath′lēt) A thrower of the bull; that is, of the verbal rather than the Iberian corrida variety.

TWELVE

GROBIANS, PHANEROMANIACS & RIPESUCKS

UNAPPEALING FOLK

Boors, slobs, sleazes and uglies

âme de boue (äm′ də bo͞o′) A "soul of mud," or somebody whose thoughts and imagination are, if not right in the gutter, no higher than the curb. The âme de boue is black-minded if not black-hearted, given to seeing the lowest or worst in anybody. A mundane, nasty, cosmically dirty mind.

badaud (bä dō′) An idle, markedly stupid individual who believes just about anything and is a half-witted gossip. Such simpletons like to hang out, satisfy curiosity and express themselves. This is something simpletons should not do. Another old word for a foolish oaf is *alcatote*. And if you've ever wanted a word for a self-confident ignoramus, the person who's not only a dimwit but one cocksure about himself or herself, go no further. It's *bayard* (a word also applied to a reddish-brown horse).

beldam (bel′dəm) A repulsive older woman or, as some more plainly put it, an ugly old hag. "Beldam" used to mean just a woman of advanced years (they evidently weren't good years for most women of advanced years). A related Scottish word is *rudas*, which means an ugly, foulmouthed old hag.

CACHINNATOR
Always a laughing matter.

cachinnator (kak′ə nā′tər) The loud laugher, whose deafening bray is usually inappropriate (the joke wasn't *that* good)—possibly because cachinnating, as the psychologists tell us, can be a symptom of hysteria. A relative of the *fleerer,* the obnoxious cachinnator emits howls of laughter chiefly to proclaim an avowed sense of humor or aroused sense of superiority.

cormorant (kôr′mə rənt) An insatiably exploitive, greedy or gluttonous person or, worse, two or three of the three. From the name of a raptorial sea bird that hawks down fish insatiably. Extreme avarice tends to be unmistakable in certain people, and the cormorant reeks of it. A predator always on the make.

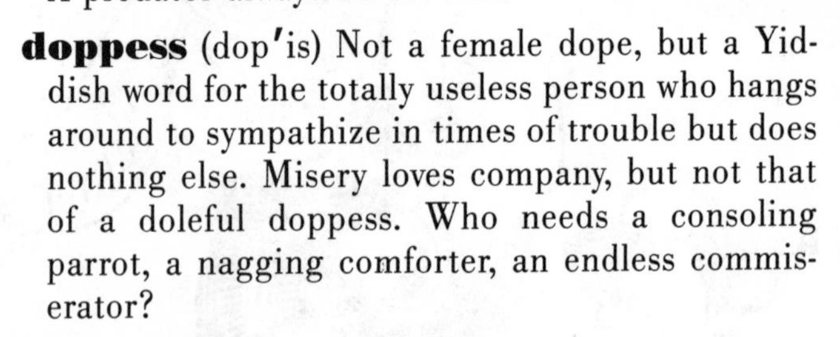

doppess (dop′is) Not a female dope, but a Yiddish word for the totally useless person who hangs around to sympathize in times of trouble but does nothing else. Misery loves company, but not that of a doleful doppess. Who needs a consoling parrot, a nagging comforter, an endless commiserator?

eructator (i ruk′tā′tər) A belcher, or a semiautomatic gas-fed eruptive vocal-popping human being. Some burp-gunners feel that articulating proper burps is as normal and healthful after a meal as saying grace before it, but society has yet to accept the wanton eructator. Like Coke, eructators come in Regular and Classic varieties.

fleerer (flēr′ər) One who is always sneering and leering, grinning and grimacing, in an ugly, mocking or derisive way. The fleerer's facial contortions and coarse sniggers are repellent, if not grotesque. Few people are worse to try to have a discreet conversation with, and few people can make enemies more quickly.

gorgon (gôr′gən) A woman whose looks are so spectacularly hideous as to be a bit terrifying, and thus an equal-rights partner for a *Quasimodo,* or male monster.

grobian (grō′bē ən) Somebody who is so coarse and slovenly as to be clownish—crude, in a word, or "rude" in older parlance. Not your cultured type, the grobian is grubby, grungy and gross. And also known as a *rudesby.*

homo trium litterarum (hō′mō trē′əm lit′-er är′əm) A "man of three letters," but not a fraternity brother or superjock. The three (Latin) letters spell *fur,* or "thief." As erudite and literary a term as you'll find for a robber, filcher, burglar, shoplifter, pickpocket or embezzler. (A pelt hi-jacker might be a fur *fur,* except that furfur means dandruff and we'd better stop right here.) A homo trium litterarum caught asportating—on the run with stolen goods—is a *backberend.* A cattle thief is an *abactor* or *abigeus.*

kvetch (kvech) or *kvetcher.* Mr. or Ms. Gripe. What else could this Yiddish word mean but a constant, irritating complainer? The kvetch gets easily bothered—about the appetizer at the restaurant, the way a meeting is being conducted, a bit of lumbago, an in-law—and lets you know with his (or her) moaning and groaning. A bitcher on wheels.

misomusist (mis′ə myo͞o′zist) Or *misosophist.* A culture revulture—the person who can't stand learning, which chiefly includes school, studying, lectures, books and instructive people. (A good teacher can spot a misomusist in no time.) Some people are happy keeping the brain away from exercise, but there's a problem with refusing knowledge, education, edification: what do you replace them with?

niddering (nid′ər ing) A coward, or the fearful, faint-of-heart individual who becomes invertebrate when bravery is called for. The anorchous (ball-less) niddering is unmellow yellow. There are all kinds of old, dusty words for a pusillanimous person, among them *recreant, caitiff, poltroon,* *craddon, quakebreech* and best of all, *quakebuttock.* But isn't niddering a particularly sniveling one? A related old word, for a skulker or shirker, is *lounderer.*

paskudnak (pos ko͞od nyok′) In plain Yiddish, somebody nasty and disgusting, possessing all the character traits thereby implied: greed, selfishness, hypocrisy, slyness, treachery. In short, a bad sort, as the British would say; or a scumbag, as Americans might say. A through-and-through bastard, to be watched closely if reluctantly.

phaneromaniac (fan′ər ə mā′nē ak) The picky person—picking compulsively at scabs or pimples or ears, scratching the scalp, or fingernailing possible wildlife on his or her own person. Most people do not enjoy watching skin-frisking phaneromaniacs in action, never knowing, or wanting to, what they'll come up with in their nervous self-scavenging.

plug-ugly (plug′ug′lē) A ruffian or gang member, asocial enough to be a true stomper of the non-Dixieland variety or to be used for roughhouse political intimidation near polling places. The word was coined in the 19th century by a group of Baltimore rowdies and originally meant, according to one source, a short spike affixed to the toe of a boot and used to kick non-plug-uglies.

puckfist (puk′fist′) A braggart, or your everyday egotistic blowhard. Nobody can be a good listener when a puckfist is doing the talking, because these windy, conceited or insecure boasters are full of themselves—and so, quickly, is everybody else. (Truthful boasting, by the way, is called jactation; false boasting, jactitation.) A big braggart is not only a puckfist but also a *cacafuego,* a *braggadocio,* a *rodomont* and a *fanfaron.* A braggart who is also a coward is a *Bobadil* (from a character in a Ben Jonson play).

rabiator (rā′bē ā′tər) Your violent, criminal type, from the schoolyard bully to the armed robber, and one with a rabid, noisy personality—not the brains behind any gang. You might call a hardened criminal a sclerotic (or indurated) rabiator.

ripesuck (rīp′suk′) A distinctively earthy term for a person who can be easily bribed. The ripesuck is squishily corrupt when it comes to under-the-table money—the "no" suddenly turns to "yes." A wallflower of avarice, just waiting to be asked. Gets along well with *boodlers.*

rixatrix (rik sā′triks) A shrewish woman, skilled in scolding, nagging, and getting shrilly on one's case. In Latin a "rixator" is a brawler. Whether because of historical sexism or not, dictionaries are filled with words for shrewish women—among them, *termagant, virago* and *Xanthippe.* Here's a vote for rixatrix, but see *catamaran* as well.

shellout-falterer (shel′out fôl′tər ər) The classic hypocrite who sort of insists on picking up the check at the end of a meal (or other social activity), but only sort of. Being slow on the draw is everything here. The adept, ever relieved shell-out-falterer is the cunning cheapskate who gets the other person to insist first—or is it last? Tried-and-true ploys include pretending not to notice the check's arrival, fumbling at length for one's wallet and picking the perfect time for a visit to the restroom. The term is from the 1950s, a variation on "fallout shelter."

shot-clog (shot′klog′) Or *shot-log.* The bore or drip whose company is tolerated because he or she pays the whole bill or a fair share of it. ("Shot" is an old word for a bill to be paid.) However boring or stupid, the person willing to pick up the tab often brings out a miraculous tolerance and appreciation in us. With a shot-clog, the main thing is always to have another friend along to make things bearable.

souteneur (so͞o′tə no͝or′) A live-in pimp, or a male "supporter" who resides with his prostitute girlfriend or wife and lives off her back-shaking earnings. Not the sort of head of household most women dream of hooking up with.

TIGHT-ASS
Priggish to the end.

tight-ass (tīt′ as′) The supremely held-in individual—circumspect, rigid, reluctant, humorless—who tightens up when others let go. In personality, a cast-iron sphincter. Tight-asses also tend to be excessively obedient and dutiful and dully goody-goody—too moral to be naughty, too hidebound to be anything but a play-it-safe employee. An authoritarian anal-retentive is not a tight-ass but a hard-ass.

trombenik (trom′bə nik) A loud, egotistical or thrasonical (boastful) bore, according to Yiddish (from an earlier Polish word for a brass horn). Trombeniks are the big winds you run into at business lunches or on blind dates and later describe as being insufferably obnoxious.

yahoo (yä′hōō) A thoroughly crass, stupid and brutish person, morally degraded and degrading to be around; a loud and conspicuous lowlife and vulgarian, from the unsavory lover of violence in movies and sports to the uncivilized, foulmouthed drunk. The original Yahoos were a race of vicious human beings in Jonathan Swift's "Gulliver's Travels." There are definitely yahoos in real life. Animals, more or less, and not yet an endangered species. A yahoo may well be one of the *canaille* (rabble) or the *faex populi* (dregs of society).

THIRTEEN

ALDIBORONTIPHOSCOPHORNIOS, BUZZWIGS & MONSTRES SACRÉS

STRICTLY HIGH-PROFILE

The egotistic, the flashy and the pompous

ALDIBORONTIPHOSCOPHORNIO
Good for pomp in any circumstance.

Aldiborontiphoscophornio (ôl′də bə ron′ tə fos′kə fôr′nē ō′) A pompous person, not in words of one syllable but in a word of 10 syllables. This is what you call a long word. And why shouldn't there be an unduly long word, or sesquipedalian, for an individual who is unduly self-inflated and pretentious? From an old English burlesque with a title just as hard to pronounce, and later used by Sir Walter Scott to tag somebody he considered worthy of the name.

autotheist (ô toth′ē ist) The individual who is not only self-centered but self-deifying, or at least self-worshiping. Feeling that God dwells not within you but at the right hand of You is about as egotistic as is humanly (or godly) possible. Know anybody who thinks he or she is a little god, or a big one?

Boanerges (bō′ə nûr′jēz) A public speaker or preacher who is megalophonous, or roaringly powerful of voice; a thundering declaimer or orator. A microphone in the hand of such a volume-voice can endanger public eardrums. Another word for Boanerges is *stentor,* and yet another is *scaldabanco* (literally, "heated bench"). A haranguer or preacher, loud or not, is a *concionater.*

bon vivant (bon′ vē vänt′) The practiced appreciator of the good things in life, or the compleat and contented high-on-the-hog liver. Bon vivants know good and abundant food and drink when they see it, and it's been noticed that most of them do not have small abdomens. If living well is the best revenge, the bon vivant enjoys platefuls and goblets of vindication.

boulevardier (bo͞ol′vär dyā′) The dapper man about town carefully turned out, sprightly of gait and ready to step out with the proper or improper female. The true Louis Jourdan or Maurice Chevalier type is harder to find these days, but among males there will always be natty cats, sauntering sharpies and breezy boulevardiers.

brahmin (brä′min) The aloof, imposingly well-bred and cultured gentleman or -woman, usually in the person of an old-money New Englander. The brahmin has breeding, taste and a certain proper remoteness. Brahmins are superior but try not to mention it to their less patrician *coevals* (contemporaries).

buzzwig (buz′wig′) A person of importance, otherwise known as a bigwig, big noise, major mover or V.I.P. A word reflecting the fact that dignified people of consequence once sported large, bushy wigs.

cockalorum (kok′ə lôr′əm) The conceited, self-important little man, or, as a line goes in an old 1950s movie, a banjo player who ate a big breakfast. Short in stature and tall in strut, the cockalorum is the puffed-up runt you can't stand at the office, the Mighty Mouse of ego now running for a local political office, the cologne-reeking bantamweight grinning up at ladies' chins at Happy Hour.

empleomaniac (em′plē ə mā′nē ak′) One hell-bent on holding public office; the eternal candidate with an ungovernable impulse to govern, for whom it is incumbent to be an incumbent. Coyly susceptible to drafts. Glad to be nominated, eager to serve, ecstatic to be reelected. Likes best to be known as a public servant; anything but a politician—or an empleomaniac. A harmlessly incompetent public officeholder is (from a character in the musical comedy "Of Thee I Sing") a *Throttlebottom.*

magnifico (mag nif′ə kō′) The person of high position or exalted station—or just of grand, impressive appearance. The most magnificos per square yard are found at coronations, state funerals and celebrity roasts.

miles gloriosus (mē′lās glôr′ē ō′səs) A boastful soldier—or sailor, Coast Guardsman or Marine, for that matter. In times of armed strife there are always war stories for the uniformed blowhard to tell. In peacetime there are training exploits, promotions, world travel and *unbelievable* three-day-pass or shore-leave conquests. The original Miles Gloriosus was a stock character in Roman drama.

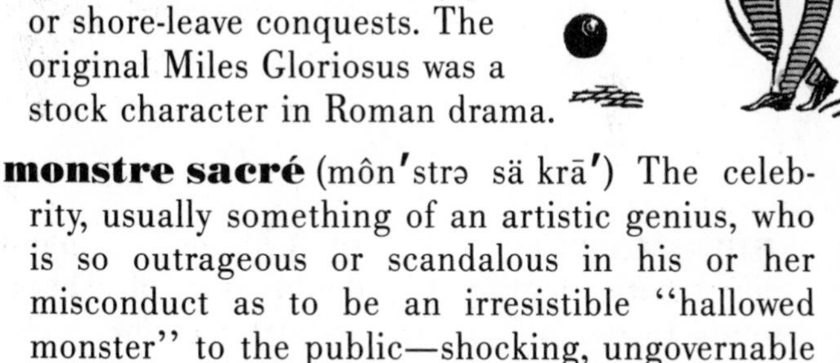

monstre sacré (môn′strə sä krā′) The celebrity, usually something of an artistic genius, who is so outrageous or scandalous in his or her misconduct as to be an irresistible "hallowed monster" to the public—shocking, ungovernable and always fun to read about.

petit maître (pə tē′ mā′trə) Not just a dandy dresser but a somewhat too elegant, prissy or even effeminate one, if nonetheless a successful ladies' man. A lapel-dusting, hair-adjusting, cuff-fussing fop.

FOURTEEN

DEMIREPS, HYPHENATES & WANGATEURS

MYSTERIOUS OR QUESTIONABLE

Ambitious types, smoothies, sly types and operators

Amphitryon (am fit′rē ən) A dinner or party host whose identity is in doubt—sort of a backwards version of a surprise party honoree. The host may choose to be anonymous because of modesty or game-playing—or a position high up on the Ten Most Wanted list. The word, from classical mythology, comes from the name of a husband whose form Zeus took in order to wine and dine the husband's wife; as a result of the evening, she gave birth to Hercules.

autothaumaturgist (ô′tō thô′mə tûr′jist) The coy or cagey person whose mission is to appear mysterious or quite remarkable; one of the slyest kinds of poseurs, avid to achieve a certain image. The autothaumaturgist likes to be considered "fascinating," and works at it.

barbae tenus sapientes (bär′bī tā′nəs sä′-pē en′tās) People who purport knowledge that in fact they don't possess; loosely, "men who are wise only as far as their beards extend." How many barbae tenus sapientes (or b.t.s.'s) there are still in this age of glib consultants, self-styled "in-depth" reporters and ponderous political and economic panel discussions!

AMPHITRYON
Faceless but gracious.

comprador (kom′prə dôr′) Anybody thought to be working for a foreign power and, worse, for that power's domination. A business person, for instance, who is a suspected agent, or that new immigrant neighbor of yours whom you once caught yodeling and who just might be secretly working for Switzerland's overthrow of the United States. (Originally, a comprador was a Chinese hired by a foreign establishment in China to handle the local employees.) A citizen who is not a seditious schemer, who is a mere fellow countryman or compatriot, is a *synethnic.* A simple foreigner is a *tramontane* or *heterochthon.*

demirep (dem′ē rep′) The woman of doubtful moral character, socially adventurous—or, as the respected Oxford English Dictionary puts it, "of suspected chastity." There seems less call today for a word for a woman who may many times over not be a virgin, who may even be a kept woman or important other. Demireps hang out in the demimonde and are also called *demimondaines.*

éminence grise (em ē näns′ grēz′) Or *gray eminence.* A person who possesses or exercises power behind the scenes; the term derives from the nickname of a crafty 17th-century monk who operated as a confidential agent for Cardinal Richelieu. Whether in government or business, the gray eminence who is black-hearted is a sneaky *cryptarch* (secret ruler) to be closely watched or distantly avoided.

faux bonhomme (fō′ bôn ôm′) The smarty hearty: one of those unbearable people who seem so amiable and jolly and who are phonies—the counterfeit good fellows. The business and professional worlds abound in faux bonhommes, of course. So do certain religious cults, self-help seminars and cocktail lounges.

faux-naïf (fō′nä ēf′) A "false innocent": one who pretends to be extremely innocent or artlessly simple but who is shrewdly faking it. Faux-naïfs are women, not born yesterday, who affect being wispy, fresh-eyed ingenues, and are also the artists or writers who coyly adopt childlike personas in their work or life. Some faux-naïfs tend to be particularly evasive about the subject of age.

girouette (zhir′o͞o et′) Not "pirouette," but a pirouetting survivor—the very unfixed, fickle person who continually changes opinions or stances to go along with what is popular. The girouette, or *weathercock,* is a trendy bendy. A particularly opportunistic changer or accommodator is a *time-server, temporizer* or *trimmer.*

highbinder (hī′bīn′dər) A shady individual engaged in corruption, fraud or swindling; in particular, a slick, pocket-lining politician. Whether profiting through a scam or a padded payroll, the highbinder cannot resist the low road.

hyphenate (hī′fə nit) A naturalized American suspected of having divided national loyalties or a sneaky preference for his or her country of origin. Not too many people today are accused of questionable patriotism, and many foreign-born inhabitants of the U.S.A. are among the strongest American patriots. But, while dated, "hyphenate" remains an interesting word—if only because it sounds less like a type of person than like a punctuation mark.

lion-hunter (lī′ən hun′tər) A famous-people groupie, eager to mingle with celebrities. Attracted by others' limelight, lion-hunters love to get invited to posh parties or do business with celebs anywhere. The lion-hunter is akin to the social climber, but here fame is the name of the game, even if it doesn't rub off.

MAWWORM & DEMIREP
Mealy Mouth meets Hot Lips.

mawworm (mô′wûrm′) Or *faux dévot.* A pious, mealy-mouthed hypocrite, whose sactimonious act is totally fraudulent. The mawworm is living proof that phony saints are far more unbearable than all-out sinners. The word comes from the name of a character in an 18th-century play, and a synonym (from the Bible) is *whited sepulcher.* A mawworm is also a type of intestinal parasite, no easier to stomach.

medicaster (med′i kas′tər) A medical charlatan, the pseudo-professional treater or healer who exploits false hopes and knows only whereof he or she bills. Gimmick treatments usually go hand in hand with medicasters, who are also called *quacksalvers* (the word from which we get "quack").

meshugener (mi sho͝og′ə nər) Any male or (*meshugena*) female who is noticeably crazy, possessed, obsessed or otherwise weirdly hung up on some fixed idea or wandering worry. Like the nutcase woman down the street who hand-delivers her mail around town to save on postage. A screw or two loose here, and it's too late for the toolbox. A short-order kook who's a tall order to handle.

plutogogue (plo͞o′tə gog′) A person who favors or represents the interests of the wealthy. In defense of plutogogues, possibly it's worth mentioning that the rich, or the *plutocrats,* are a minority group of sorts.

rastacouère (räs′tä kwâr′) A foreigner whose title, claims of wealth or such are suspect, maybe spurious or ill-gotten. A foreign arriviste or parvenu. Is she a bogus countess or the real thing? Until the truth is in, she's neither. She's a rastacouère.

schlockmeister (shlok′mī′stər) Someone who sells or deals in junk of any variety, who is drawn to purveying things that are quisquilian, or trashy. Both the retailer of cheap "Souvenir of Atlanta" barometers made in Hong Kong and the publisher of trashy romance novels are schlockmeisters. Schlockmeisters consider potential profits without worrying too much about details like quality or good taste, though most of them are infrunite—lacking good taste to begin with.

Svengali (sfen gä'lē) A usually evil manipulator, one using a strong personal influence, if not satanic powers, to compel another to do his or her bidding. A very serious bad influence, and probably getting worse. Svengalis (the original was an evil hypnotist in George du Maurier's novel "Trilby") materialize as sinister political advisers, shady personal business managers and cunningly exploitive spouses. You don't want a Svengali pulling strings for you, as they'll be your strings.

wangateur (wang'gə to͝or') A voodoo conjurer. A Louisiana word that possibly should be adopted by all other 49 states. Possible meanings here, from the look and the sound of the word, are Chinese, sexual, collegian—just about anything you can conjure up. A person who works miracles without necessarily resorting to voodoo is a *thaumaturgist, theurgist* or *mirabiliary.*

FIFTEEN

CUCKQUEANS, MAMMOTHREPTS & PENTHERAPHOBES

STRICTLY FAMILY

Relatives, in-laws, children, singles and cheaters

affine (ə fīn′) An in-law, or any relative whom through mere marriage you have acquired, earned, valued or put up with. Announcing that your affines are coming this weekend will impress other people that you're expecting an important delivery.

agnate (ag′nāt) Your dad's brother (or your uncle), sister (your aunt), father (your grandpa) and mother (your grandma) are all agnates, being relatives on your paternal side; as a group, the *patrikin.* Uncle Ted especially likes you to call him a handsome agnate because he thinks you're saying "magnate."

backfisch (bäk′fish′) An adolescent girl in her mid-teens and one who is still a bit immature, or swimming upstream toward womanhood. In the German from which the word comes to us, a "fish to bake or fry."

bedswerver (bed′swûr′vər) A husband or wife who is unfaithful, or a spouse who speaks fluent pillow talk to an extramarital acquaintance. Also known as an *advouterer* (or *advouteress*) or a *spousebreak.*

burdalane (bûr′də lān) A last, surviving child. An English word for the Scottish phrase *burd alane,* or "quite alone."

by-blow (bī′blō′) Or *by-child.* A bastard in the legitimate sense—of the illegitimate-child variety. (Presumably, a long English novel about the fortunes of a child born out of wedlock would be a blow-by-blow by-blow account.) Other exotic synonyms for offspring of mysterious parentage abound in dictionaries: *adulterine, filium nullius, bantling, avetrol, filius populi, woods colt* and the ever popular Yiddishism, *momser.*

contubernal (kən to͞o′bər nəl) A person who lives together with somebody else, or an intimate companion. Originally, a contubernal was some body who shared a tent with another, back in the days when people said "Your tent or mine?" (A simple tent dweller, without a roommate, is a *Rechabite,* which can also refer to an abstainer from alcohol.) The contubernal who is shacking up with a person of the opposite sex is also a *POSSLQ (Person of Opposite Sex Sharing Living Quarters).*

cornute (kôr no͞ot′) A cuckold, or a husband whose wife has an extramarital hobby named Tom, Dick or Harry.

cuckquean (kuk′wē ən) A woman with an unfaithful husband; the female equivalent of a *cuckold.* An odd word, as henlike as cuckold is roosterlike, but do you know another single word for a wife who is being cheated on?

digamist (dig′ə mist) Or *deuterogamist.* A man or a woman who is married for the second time, whether out of habit or because of an abiding optimism. An extremely impatient digamist is, of course, a bigamist.

DILLING
Last but not least.

dilling (dil′in) A last-born or youngest child, and especially a boy or girl who is somewhat frail and the darling of Mom and Dad; the weakling of the litter, so to speak. (A first-born child is an *eigne* or *firstling;* a frail infant who dies within one month of birth is a *chrisom child.*) But then there's always sibling rivalry, and the favored dilling (also called a *toshence*) is not always a darling to older brubs and sisses.

enate (ē′nāt) Any relative on one's mother's side. If he or she is also staunchly on the mother's side in family wrangles, he or she could be said to be an innate enate. A whole mother-loving cluster of enates is known as a *matrikin.*

gravida (grav′i də) A pregnant woman, and a term modifiable by a number or prefix according to how many times she has been pregnant. A woman expecting her fourth child, for example, is either a *4-gravida* or a *quadragravida.* A woman who has never given birth is a *nulligravida,* and one pregnant for the first time is a *primagravida* or *unigravida.*

henhussy (hen′huz′ē) A husband or live-in male who busies himself with housework more commonly done by women. Not a nice-sounding word for the modern house-husband, but for some women the henhussy is the true man around the house—one who has no ego or identity problem. Two other words for henhussy are *cotquean* and *betty.*

mammothrept (mam′ə thrept′) An overindulged child, especially one raised by a grandmother. Which may suggest that in a generation-gap showdown, an infant will always get the better of a grandma. A spoiled child can also be called a *cade* or an *enfant gâté.* Whatever name they go by, pampered youngsters are no fun as charges for a *bersatrix,* or babysitter.

multipara (mul tip′ə rə) A woman who has borne more than one child (on more than one occasion), or a mother several times over. As in the case of "gravida," referring to pregnancy rather than birth itself, there are related words here: *secundipara* for a mother who has given birth twice, *tripara* for one who has achieved this three times. The mother of twins is a *gemellipara.*

HENHUSSY
The man around the house.

pentheraphobe (pen′thə rə fōb′) The individual with a strong fear, dislike or general aversion to his or her mother-in-law. Any study of comedy material, divorces and family homicides over the past hundred years strongly suggests that pentherophobia is not a rare condition. Then there's the *soceraphobe,* a more extreme case, who dislikes both in-laws.

quatrayle (kwot′rāl) A great-great-great grandfather. Everybody has quatrayles, but few get to have one who's still alive. On the other hand, what could be more useful than a simple, nine-letter word for one's father's father's father's father? A quatrayle is a real forefather. A mere great-great-grandfather is a *tresayle.*

relict (rel′ikt) A surviving person, especially a widow. In order not to suggest that she is a fossil, it is important here to pronounce the final *t.* More generally, a relict is a survivor of a vanishing race, species or the like.

tocophobe (tō′kō fōb′) A woman who dreads childbirth—or her husband who does also, for that matter. Most tocophobes have not yet had a child and are apprehensive about the graduation ceremony from being a *unigravida.* Some are already mothers but still (with good reason) dread labor pains. A tocophobe, or *maieusiophobe,* should probably know a good *levatrice* (midwife).

vitricophobe (vit′ri kə fōb′) The person fearful of a stepfather. The vitricophobe feels that the new man in Mother's life has made a step in the wrong direction: closer. And a stepmother? If you're not wild about her, you're a *novercaphobe.*

SIXTEEN

HOYDENS, PORNOGENARIANS & TETNITS

THE YOUNG, THE OLD

The green, the precocious, the late and the crotchety

alter kocker (ôl′tər kok′ər) A canny, stubborn old man who has been around but has ended up as mostly an old fart. Or shrewd buzzard. Sometimes he hasn't been around as much as he'd like on women's bodies and still has a rheumy eye and bony hand for the girls. The second word here in the Yiddish is related to the more familiar word "kaka."

Darby and Joan (där′bē ən jōn′) An old and extremely happy married couple. The English gave us this double term, but we can certainly use one for a twosome who maintain (or attain) conjugal felicity at an advanced age. Couples who do not become Darby-and-Joans may become Mutt-and-Jeffs or Punch-and-Judys.

grig (grig) A lively and light-hearted, small or young person; a blithe sprite or little bundle of energy, usually appreciated in a family that has its share of drones, stiffs, pigs and scuzzes. Often used in the phrase "merry grig."

grisard (griz′ərd) A gray-haired person. (A gray-bearded person is, simply, a *graybeard*.) We hear much of blondes and brunettes and redheads and baldies but little about grisards, who suffer from poliosis, or grayness of hair, and some of whom are under 35 and may hire a *canitist,* or hair tinter. A gray area, perhaps. An old gray-haired or white-haired man is a *hoarhead.*

grognard (grōn yär′) An old soldier—the true seasoned veteran, and especially one who is a grumbling grouser (as were the men of Napoleon's Old Guard, to whom the word was originally applied). The military bearing may be a bit bent over, but the grognard's memories are battle-ready.

hobbledyhoy (hob′əl dē hoi′) A clumsy stripling; the awkward, gawky and callow adolescent male who is galumphing somewhere between boyhood and manhood—who seems to be all knees, all elbows, all neck and, at times, all finger in the nose. Just as tomboys often become beauties, many hunks were once hobbledyhoys. The hobbledyhoy is ephebic—entering manhood.

hoyden (hoi′dən) A brash and boisterous upstart of a girl, the kind of wild tomboy who used to be called a romp. Irrepressible and precociously liberated, the hoyden is an Annie Oakley in her approach to life and parents. The rare young lady kicked out of a rare girls' boarding school is sometimes an unmanageable, clowning hoyden.

hunks (hungks) A male who's a living burst of sex appeal? Not here. The hunks (singular) is a crusty, bad-humored old man, and a very stingy one. Herman Melville never called a sailor a hunk, but he did call one or two a hunks, as they were surly misers.

neonate (nē′ə nāt′) A newborn child, up to about a month old, or a 30-day wonder of the procreative rather than the military type. Parents are thrilled with their neonates, and politicians like to kiss them. But somebody greeting a mother of newborn twins with "What a cute and healthy pair of neonates you've got there!" might be asking for trouble.

Nestor (nes′tər) An old man worthy to be revered for his wisdom as a patriarch, having not only lived a long time but also managed to observe and absorb life as few others have. The opinion of a Nestor should be valued by the young, and by geezers, coots, crones, bats and fogies as well.

nymphet (nim fet′) A sexually precocious girl just into her teenage years, if not yet into trouble. Like the famed bubblegum temptress of Vladimir Nabokov's "Lolita"—who in fact was prepubescent when Humbert Humbert was first smitten with her—the nymphet has grown up almost fast enough for the older males under her hormonal spell.

opsigamist (op sig′ə mist) The man or woman who takes that single step late in life and finally marries. Newspapers like it when one opsigamist marries another; they also like it when a male opsigamist marries a sweet young thing (the pairing called a *December and May*) or a female opsigamist weds a "boy who could be her son!"

opsimath (op′si məth′) The older person—better late than never—who begins to study or to learn late in life; possibly a refreshing contrast to the person who thinks that he or she has damn well learned everything early in life. Some opsimaths are latter-day readers, musicians, hobbyists and second-careerists. Others, as senior scholars, get truly advanced degrees.

pornogenarian (pôr′nə jə nâr′ē ən) A dirty old man (D.O.M.), or an elderly lecher in whom the flesh may be weak but the spirit and, sometimes, the hands are a bit too willing. A scuzzy-duddy. Pornogenarians include libidinous duffers who are quadragenarians, quinquagenarians, septuagenarians, octogenarians, nonagenarians and, of course, sexagenarians.

rareripe (râr′rīp′) Anybody who (like the fruits or vegetables to which the word was originally applied) is an early bloomer, precocious mentally, emotionally or physically. An earthy synonym (and a word used by President Lincoln) for prodigy, one who is young but no greenhorn.

scuddy (skud′ē) A naked child or bare-ass babe. Scuddies should be kept mostly indoors, as nobody likes to see a muddy scuddy.

TETNIT
A late delivery.

tetnit (tet′nit) A geriatric-boom baby, or a child born to parents who are relatively old. Which means that by the time their hale young tetnit is a *tanquam,* or ready for college, the proud parents will be near or beyond retirement and definitely not planning any more tetnits.

twichild (twī′chīld′) A *dotard,* or an old person who has lost a certain mental sharpness or has reached the state of dotage, often called a second childhood. A twichild can be difficult to deal with. But that second childhood? The senior citizen in question may be enjoying it even more than the first.

wunderkind (vo͝on′dər kind′) The person who is dazzlingly successful or brilliantly gifted or skilled at a relatively young age—the musical prodigy, the mathematics or chess whiz, the meteorically risen and youthful CEO of a large corporation. One whose genus is genius.

SEVENTEEN

EYESERVANTS, NEPOTISTS & SINECURISTS

WORKERS AND SHIRKERS

Bosses, opportunists, robots, loafers and backbiters

airmonger (âr′mong′gər) The man or woman who is attracted to visionary ideas and projects. Rather than keeping their feet on the ground, airmongers prefer leaps of the imagination, inventive notions, future possibilities. A city surrounded by waterfalls? A sure-fire diet based on maximum consumption of chocolate? The perfect mousetrap? These are the stuff of an airmonger's dreams.

chairwarmer (châr′wôr′mər) The employee who does or contributes little except warmth to the chair he or she occupies. The settled-in but superfluous slacker or do-nothing. Chairwarmers are typically senior people, unjustly ensconced and perpetuated.

ergophile (ûr′gə fīl′) The person who just loves working and is lax about relaxing—more recently known as the *workaholic*. The ergophile thrives on exertion, deadline pressure, long hours and all those things most of us work hard to avoid: forging ahead, buckling down, grinding away. The prospect of sudden leisure time may leave him or her at a loss.

ergophobe (ûr′gə fōb′) Or *ergasiophobe.* Somebody mightily averse to work, or interested in making everything but an effort. Numerous ergophobes are happily unemployed, but far more are bluffing things out beautifully in the workplace, hopscotching between coffee breaks, phone calls, lunch marathons and long visits with the crossword puzzle to the restroom. (Chronic sloughers haven't yet gotten ergophobia acknowledged as a vocational disability to be indulged and recompensed, but they're working on it.) Somebody afraid of being *over*worked is a *ponophobe.*

eyeservant (ī′sûr′vənt) The person who works or is dutiful only while being watched; the out-of-sight, out-of-minding employee whose exertion extends only to putting in an appearance. One's own lookout when it comes to expected effort. The brother or sister to the clock-watcher: the boss-watcher.

fainéant (fā′nē ənt) Literally, a do-nothing: a stylish French term for an irresponsibly lazy or idle person, the chronic sluggard with lots of sit-down-and-stay. In the workplace, the otiose fainéant is one of the *chairwarmers.*

idiopraxist (id′ē ō prak′sist) The enterprising individual who puts ideas into practice—who not only talks a good game but schedules and plays the game, as it were. Any good organization needs such industrious implementers. More autonomous idiopraxists include inventors, successful dieters and habit breakers, and those remarkable innovators hailed as pioneers.

levanter (lə van′tər) An adult runaway, or one who has elected to blow town because of a bet lightly made or a debt heavily hanging, who has maybe pulled a fast one on the wrong person. Gangster movies are full of nervous levanters, or *lamsters,* who double-cross somebody and get fearfully active in a geographical way. A levanter is also a strong easterly wind in the Mediterranean. The human levanter blows any which way but soon.

martinet (mär′tə net′) The rigid, whip-cracking superior or boss, otherwise known as the office tyrant or royal bastard. (General Jean Martinet was a strict French disciplinarian.) The martinet is living proof that authoritarians are not majoritarians, or people concerned about the votes or wishes of the membership. While some bosses are father figures and others pussy cats, the martinet runs things strictly according to the clock, the book and the bottom line. He or she often gets results. He or she also often gets the undying hatred of the employees. An out-and-out cruel taskmaster who is mastiphoric (carrying a whip) is a *Simon Legree.*

myrmidon (mûr′mi don′) One of those subordinates, or hirelings, who do anything and everything asked of them—but to such an unquestioning degree that their obedience becomes less an admirable show of loyalty than a staunchly mindless, pitiless carrying out of orders. The myrmidon is a flunky, and an ardent, frightening eagerbeaver of one. The original myrmidons were the trusted, warlike subjects of Achilles who fought for him in the Trojan War.

nepotist (nep′ə tist) The employer who doesn't hesitate to hire nephews—or nieces, brothers, sisters, aunts, uncles, grandchildren or in-laws. For the nepotist, business is family, and relative newcomers to the staff are always welcome, qualified or not. Blood is thicker than résumés.

new broom (no͞o′ bro͞om′) The new boss or superior who wastes no time in making his or her presence or changes felt, who is maybe a little too zealous in the new position of authority. Some new brooms try to make clean sweeps and are regarded by the dusty old-timers as people who should be riding their brooms.

nihilarian (nī′ə lâr′ē ən) A person who deals with things of no importance, whose concerns are a niggling and nugatory (trifling) affair. The office worker saddled with keeping records of inconsequential details or (an *alimenter*) feeding a machine, the seller of a worthless or meaningless item, the disgruntled gofer, the subordinate who never gets to be part of the real action—these are helpless nihilarians, some of whom know it all too well ("I have a nothing job"). Many people who deal with matters of no import are not conscious of that fact. They're still nihilarians.

panjandrum (pan jan′drəm) A grandly self-important personage or official; above all, a local *magnifico*, or high-profile bigwig, with pretensions. The panjandrum not only holds office or petty power but revels in all the vainglory of being a (swelled) head of something. Prevalant panjandrums include certain mayors, sheriffs, muckamucks of fraternal organizations, and part-time generals.

proneur (prō no͝or′) A subordinate or colleague prone to proffering nothing but praise—in Yiddish a *tochis lecher* and in plain American an ass-kisser. This is the constant flatterer, the burnished brown-nose, popular only with those whose buttocks they embrace—and sometimes not even with them. Another word for a toadyish person always currying favor is *pickthank*.

puisne (pyo͞o′nē) Any subordinate or junior employee. And an interesting, not to say tricky, term

PANJANDRUM & PUISNES
A catered-to affair.

to use for a lesser member of an organization because it's pronounced exactly like its offshoot, "puny."

sinecurist (sī′nə kyŏŏr′ist) The lucky stiff, also called a *feather merchant,* with a criminally easy, almost effortless vocation—whether a cushy job, a dream appointment or a breeze for a responsibility. Most sinecurists are quiet about their lucky slot because they're afraid others will feel resentful. They're right.

EIGHTEEN

BEAU-NASTIES, BUN-DUSTERS & LOUNGE LIZARDS

ONLY MALES

Womanizers, chauvinists, weaklings and duds

beau-nasty (bō′nas′tē) A contradiction in appearance if not in terms, the beau-nasty is the fellow who is finely dressed but visibly dirty. A soiled sport. Only the beau-nasty looks simultaneously natty and tatty.

benedict (ben′ə dikt) Or *benedick.* A newly married man, and especially one who was a longtime bachelor. (A change of heart after the ceremony would make him, one would guess, an Arnold Benedict.) Named for a character in Shakespeare's "Much Ado About Nothing," the benedict is either a man who has seen the light at the end of the aisle or a nuptial holdout who has weakened and capitulated. In most cases, he achieved his new status with the help of a *paranymph* (best man) and some *anteambules* (ushers).

bun-duster (bun′dus′tər) An effete male who likes to go to teas or similar mild social occasions, mostly for, well, the cake and cookies (he is also known as a *cake-eater* or *cookie-pusher*). Bun-dusters tend to be rather selfish wimps who don't reward their hosts or hostesses with electrifying conversation, much less wit. A face-feeding, often effeminate *gâteau*-crasher.

carpet knight (kär′pət nit′) A man—not too admired—who devotes himself to sheer idleness, comfort and pleasure around a woman or women. A kind of stay-at-home, emasculated soldier. The word says it: he should be out there righting wrongs, getting a job or at least mowing the lawn instead of lolling lazily in the boudoir or distressing the damsel he's living off. Shouldn't he?

cicisbeo (chi′chiz bā′ō) The lover or escort of a married woman (and a word originally applied to amorous gallants of 18th-century Italy). The young architect who's being increasingly seen with unhappily married Mrs. DuCamp at gallery openings? Or Steve, who's been seen repeatedly in the back row of the local movie house nibbling popcorn off Alice M.'s shoulder while Joe M. is out of town? Cheeky cicisbeos both. Lovers? Or just friends?

ctenophile (ten′ə fīl′) The comb lover, especially the back-pocket male variety. Serious carriers of plastic or rubber hair-rakes tend to dawdle before restroom mirrors, combing and coifing and patting to get the look just right. Not all ctenophiles are leather-jacketed guys from the 1950s.

dapperling (dap′ər ling) A diminutive, well-groomed male or, as the major dictionaries echo one another, "a dapper little fellow." So the dapperling is a short guy but also a dressy, noticeable one. A small dandy.

flaneur (flä nŏŏr′) An idle, lazy, lounging or sauntering man-about-town, something of a useless swell or creepy playboy. A flaneur is also an intellectual trifler, the dilettante who dips into this or that to no greater purpose than passing amusement. When two flaneurs (of either type) get together, it's often an occasion of great mutual indifference. The female here is a *flaneuse.*

good old boy (go͝od′ ōl boi′) The y'all male who is a solid Southerner in roots and outlook, and to his fellow Confederate males a loyal buddy and rascal. The image of the good old boy is not one of great education and refinement, though there are wealthy and successful grass-roots Rebs aplenty, and maybe even yuppie good old boys.

gynecomast (gī′nə kō mast′) The boy or man whose breasts are large and noticeable enough to be considered womanish. Gynecomasts are often on the chubby side and, as youngsters, do not have an easy time of it in locker rooms or at the beach with their less bathycolpian (deep-bosomed) mates. The gynecomast usually wishes he were planistethic, or flat-chested.

lounge lizard (lounj′ liz′ərd) The kind of slick, slithering creep and womanizer who's found hovering around darkened bars in midafternoon, or any self-styled charmer of females whose behavior is devious and tacky. The lounge lizard makes more pickups than an old phonograph arm. He's also a sexual freeloader, who cagily ends up being entertained at a woman's apartment rather than shelling out for a more legitimate date. This is a slimeball slouch, philandering parasite and sleazy Lothario; a lecher and cheapskate rolled into one. The lounge lizard always knows his place—hers.

meacock (mē′kok′) An original Mr. Milquetoast: a man who is weak, cowardly, uxorious (or wife-subservient), lackluster—take your pick. A major wimp if not, like the *mollycoddle,* one who is that way because of being spoiled. Despite the meatily suggestive elements of the word, its origin is unknown.

MOLLYCODDLE
Mama's boy forever.

mollycoddle (mol′ē kod′əl) Or *namby-pamby.* A man or boy who has been pampered and has grown, or not grown, to be a weak or effeminate milksop. When people detect somebody who has had far too easy an early life, as the mollycoddle has, they're likely to give him a hard further life. Your basic immature, overprotected sissy.

peladophobe (pi lā′də fōb′) The man who worries about going bald—whose hairs are really splitting on him. With countless head-rethatching remedies on the market, the bald fact is that there are many peladophobes around. The peladophobe has either a climbing forehead, a widening bald spot or a whole head fighting a losing battle for the Thin Black Lines. Hair losers often avoid overhead lights, depend on careful strand arrangement and become sporty hat collectors.

phallocrat (fal′ə krat′) Or *androcrat.* The rampant male chauvinist; the *Homo erectus* who will have none of this women's-rights stuff. Whether overbearing husbands, self-styled man's mans, or executives who tyrannize female workers, phallocrats think that MCP is an additive to Chinese dishes. A female supremacist? A *gynecocrat.*

spado (spā′dō) A man who is impotent—categorically, as this is a legal term (and can also mean a castrated person, who is an even more jeopardized social member). Males with this problem are sometimes understandably defensive. Likewise, some females, who don't like limp excuses, believe in calling a spado a spado.

wittol (wit′əl) The man who knows that his wife is being unfaithful but who isn't especially bothered by it; not just a cuckold but a contented one. Such a mouse of a spouse is deemed an awesome idiot by acclamation, as husbands are not supposed to be quite this liberal. A wittol is also known as a *mari complaisant,* and the word also means, not astonishingly, half-wit.

BALABUSTA
Mrs. Clean.

NINETEEN

BALABUSTAS, CACKLE-BROADS & MOUSEBURGERS

ONLY FEMALES

Vixens, bombshells, teasers, crones and castrators

bacchante (bə kan′tē) A frenzied woman, as at a rousing orgy or let-it-all-hang-out cult ceremony. A bacchante (after Bacchus, the god of revelry and wine) can also be called a *maenad,* or just a wild and crazy gal. When a woman really lets her hair down, men are often eager to watch.

balabusta (bol′ə bôs′tə) This is Superhousewife: the mean-clean woman who was born to keep an immaculate, sparkling household with well-fed inhabitants. She cooks up a storm, scours up a white tornado, does everything but dry-cleaning. When floor-wax commercials aren't made at a studio, they're made at the clinical (look for plastic slipcovers) home of a balabusta. Such a useful Yiddish word for such a majestic domestic.

bas bleu (bä blo͝o′) A learned woman, theoretically, but more likely a female book-waver who is either a dilettante or a pedant and can also be called a *femme savante* or *bluestocking* ("bas bleu" is the blue stocking worn by the first such self-consciously literary ladies at their get-togethers). Look for this bookish poseur (or poseuse, as she might correct) at your local library, campus lecture or poetry group.

bona-roba (bō'nə rō'bə) A flashy loose woman, otherwise known as a scarlet woman, "showy wanton" or *Athanasian wench.* (If she is loose enough, she qualifies as a hands-down, back-down prostitute.) "Bona-roba" (from Italian, "good stuff") sounds nice enough to be taken as a courtly compliment, but this bona-roba is the woman at parties that makes husbands spill the dip and wives glare.

cackle-broad (kak'əl brôd') The wealthy and fashionable society woman who talks in the way that such women do, at cotillions, teas, lawn parties and polo matches: in the language formerly known as Scarsdale lockjaw and perpetuated along Philadelphia's Main Line. A highfalutin rich dame.

Coelebs's wife (sē'leb zəz wīf') The perfect, ideal, fantasy wife as envisioned by a day- or nightdreaming bachelor. A term that entered dictionaries from the 1809 novel "Coelebs in Search of a Wife" by Hannah Moore. Bachelors can sometimes be stingy about giving a woman a perfect ten. Sometimes a Coelebs's wife is finally found but turns out to be already Tom's, Dick's or Harry's wife.

demi-vierge (dem'ē vyerzh') The suggestive, seemingly sexual schoolgirl or young woman who is always coming on but not coming forth, quite. A "half-virgin" with, say, a seductive laugh, racy language and loose blouse but who doesn't really come to play (or vice versa). The demi-vierge somehow keeps her honor intact. Not necessarily a zipless tease; just a staunch protector of home plate.

Dresden shepherdess (drez'dən shep'ər dis) A young woman who is extremely fragile and delicate in appearance and constitution, like one of the famous china figurines from that city. To become or remain a "frail" who is so truly frail, it helps not to be in construction work and to live in a quiet country house surrounded by gardens.

femme du monde (fäm′ do͞o mônd′) The worldly woman or female sophisticate; a lady who has "been around" in the admired, classy way. Like the (male) *homme du monde,* the femme du monde is appreciably educated, traveled and perceptive about people and possibly about business, too. She is a woman's woman.

flibbertigibbet (flib′ər tē jib′it) The restlessly airy and giddy type of girl or woman who is always chattering and gossiping, or who used to be too readily summed up as a flighty female. ("I was," Joan Collins has said of her early years as an actress, "a flibbertigibbet.") Flibbertigibbets (or *giglets, flirtigigs* or *fizgigs*) haven't yet taken flight from the earth; they are still around, talking up a storm in the high school corridor or over vodka-and-tonics at a weekend party. Half of all teenage girls, according to teenage boys, are flibbertigibbets.

fag hag (fag′ hag′) The woman who likes to keep company with *urnings,* or male homosexuals, or sort of a Camp follower—and not necessarily a hag at all. Many fag hags love witty or bitchy men and find most of them to be of the other persuasion; they also love gossip, much preferring the gay dope to the straight dope (meaning the lowdown, not the person). Others just want male friends whom they can feel more at ease with because they're always being hassled sexually by heteros. (At least, they say they are.)

jolie-laide (zhô′lē led′) The woman who is plainly plain but who wins over everybody with her charm, intelligence and bright personality. A term ("pretty-ugly") that reminds us what a premium has always been placed on a woman's looks. Are winsome wallflowers born or are they made? Whichever, the jolie-laide is the lady whose company both men and women enjoy and whom kids wish they had as an aunt.

mouseburger (mous′bûr′gər) Your fairly average young woman who becomes a *real* go-getter; a gritty female careerist who—neither brilliant nor beautiful—has the quick perceptions, street smarts, willingness to sacrifice, impatient individuality and useful modesty to make it to the top. The mouseburger also has a strong, if not obvious, sex drive. Sleeping with the boss is not necessarily a no-no. Success, love and happiness are all. According to the book "Having It All" by Helen Gurley Brown, who coined the word, you're a mouseburger if you're "like a little forest animal . . . quick and adaptable. You 'know' things."

spoffokins (spof′ə kinz) A lady of the night pretending to be a queen for a day—or a whore pretending to be a wife. Numerous on-the-road husbands and traveling salesmen are happy to find a proxy doxy as a wifely stand-in for a night or two if they can't come up with a farmer's daughter. In her own way, the spoffokins tries to make a hit, almost as good as a missus. She is never made an honest woman; she's just made.

sylph (silf) A woman so slender and graceful in form and movement as to have an airy, nymphlike quality about her. An irresistibly lovely thin girl—

a nubile ectomorph, or the young Audrey Hepburn, if you will—who carries herself beautifully but completely naturally. Sylphs eat little. Some, when they get older, get ethereal sclerosis. A young or small sylph is a *sylphid.*

volva (vol′vä) This is a wise woman, one informative not only about the present but also about the future. In the days of Norse mythology she was a sapient seeress who shook, rattled and rolled bones. Today's volva is either a sage old Italian grandmother or a fortuneteller, psychic or astrologer. The word should not (but probably will) be confused with a similar word that is anatomical in meaning.

BORBORYGMITE
A four-letter man.

TWENTY

BORBORYGMITES, LEXIPHANESES & MONOGLOTS

TALKERS

Arguers, bull-throwers, literati and pronouncers

aolist (ā′ə list) Or *aedist.* A person who claims to be inspired—to feel within that sudden wind of genius or artistic urgency. The wind is sometimes more like a draft. Aolists include people who are vociferous about "the" book they will write, self-proclaimed songwriters and some who abruptly wax religious. (One who speaks in tongues is a *glossolalist.*) People who think they're inspired but who are certifiably crazy? *Entheomaniacs.*

battologist (ba tol′ə jist) The mouth who unnecessarily says the same thing over and over, reiterating (iterating, that is) to an annoying degree. The battologist not only beats a dead horse but always uses the same whip, constantly harping on what probably wasn't worth saying in the first place. An uttering bore, who can also be called a *verbigerator* or *obganiator.*

borborygmite (bôr′bə rig′mīt) A dirty mouth, or practitioner of spurcitious—foul and obscene—language. The borborygmite uses lots of four-letter words but, predictably, with ever decreasing shock value. The word is from "borborygm" or "borborygmus," which means a rumbling in the bowels (or tummy). The scurrilous language of the borborygmite is, cleanly put, aeschrolalia or coprolalia. Another name for a person with a blue vocabulary is *Thersites,* after a reviling character in Shakespeare's "Troilus and Cressida."

cacoepist (kak′ō ep′ist) A bad pronouncer of words. For every foreigner who mispronounces an English word, there are at least 17 Americans who do, one of whom might be your daughter's new English teacher. This is not to rule out the pronunciations' being amusing, too. Most families have at least one much appreciated cacoepist, and among American presidents it has been a tradition for decades to mispronounce "nuclear."

cacographer (ka kog′rə fər) A terrible speller, or a writer whose English seems to be written phonetically or modeled on the spellings of restroom graffiti. Many a good conversationalist or skilled novelist who takes pencil in hand is revealed to be a hopeless cacographer. Cacographers are probably born, not made, so this is one bad spell that's likely to persist.

deipnosophist (dīp nos′ə fist) A comfortable and agreeable table-talker; the good, interesting dinner conversationalist regardless of the cooking. (A person who is a good conversationalist generally is a *causeur* or *confabulator.* A table companion with or without the gift of gab is a *commensal* or *convictor.*) Like a good wine, a deipnosophist or two can enhance a dining experience, maybe even aid the digestion, and should not be wasted at the table where people are so busy squabbling and gorging that one never gets to dissert.

ergotist (ûr′gə tist) The slippery, pedantic user of logic—or seeming logic—in arguing. From the ergotist you hear not so much whos, whats and hows as whences, consequentlys and it-follows-thats. An overeager reasoner with an ergo ("therefore") problem. A tricky or devious persuader, of course, is a *sophist,* and one who reasons falsely about morals is a *casuist.*

facticide (fak′tə sīd′) The "killer" of facts—by twisting or distorting them for personal ends or convenience. ("Facticide" also means the fact-perverting itself.) Whenever we encounter distorted information, half-truths, doctored data or white lies, we might remember that somebody somewhere had to soften the original hard facts. The butler didn't do it. The facticide did.

heterophemist (het′ə rə fē′mist) The slip-of-the-tonguester, or one who says something other than what was intended. The slip may be Freudian ("Let's eat in and get an order of Chinese make-out") or just any inadvertent, similar-sounding word or curious reversal of syllables. (A general ungrammared abuser of English is a *solecist,* and the mishearing or mangling of speech is otosis.) Thank God for the heterophemist. What would life be without the people who give us boners, malapropisms, spoonerisms, unconscious puns and fractured English?

laudator temporis acti (lou dä′tôr tem′pə-ris äk′tē) A mouthful, but a familiar character: the one who is always extolling the good old days, the full-speed memory-lane driver (in reverse gear). "Where are the snows of yesteryear?" We may knock Archie Bunker, but sooner or later we all begin to get misty-eyed about the past and sound like l.t.a.'s. If you have a condition of aggravated nostalgia, you have nostomania. If it's just a yearning for the good old days, it's hesternopathia.

lexiphanes (lek sif′ə nēz′) Mix one swelled head with one inflated vocabulary: a person given to pretentious, bombastic words and phrases, or whose verbal philosophy is one of sesquipedalianism (long-worditis), periphrasis (beating around the bush) and obscurantism (keeping them guessing). The more hip lexiphanes is the one who expatiates with lingua in malar pouch, or talks tongue-in-cheek. Obviously, many of the words in this book are lexiphanic, for which no hollow apology will be made here.

logodaedalus (lôg′ə ded′ə ləs) Or *logodaedalist.* A wordsmith or one cleverly playful with words; the verbal sharpie, who creates and uses words with telling effectiveness. A brilliant wit is often a logodaedalus. So is a provocative poet or lyricist, a terrific punster, a jive-ass master of backtalk (or "the dozens") and especially somebody with a gift for coining words ("Time" magazine is a collective logodaedalus). In English literature, there is not a logodaedalus-of-logodaedali. There are two, Shakespeare and Joyce.

logomachist (lô gom′ə kist) The verbal stickler who likes to argue about words themselves: "Well, what do you *mean* by 'liberalism'?" The logomachist eagerly gets into the terminology of argument and likes to check the dictionary. When you hear "That depends on your definition of..." you know you're in the presence of a word-examining logomachist.

monoglot (mon′ə glot′) A speaker or knower of only one language, stolidly unilingual. It is nice to be a multilingual person, or *polyglot,* but our planet is inhabited mostly by resigned monoglots, who when traveling depend on the aid of considerate polyglots. (A speaker of two languages is a *diglottist* or *utraquist.*) Some monoglots are extreme cases and speak in not only words of one tongue but words of one syllable. The amazing linguist who is conversant with virtually all languages is a *pantoglot.*

paraphrast (par′ə frast′) One of those conversationalists always paraphrasing their own words; that is, a paraphraser, who repeats things but in different ways, which is to say, he or she expresses the meaning in yet another fashion, or, as it were, simplifies and rephrases the sentence or sentences in order to clarify, in a word, by paraphrasing.

PARAPHRAST
"In other words . . ."

prolocutor (prō lok′yə tər) A spokesperson, or anybody chosen to speak for another or others. (An *interlocutor* is a participant in a conversation or dialogue.) A resented prolocutor is usually called a mouthpiece. A very special kind of prolocutor is the *engastrimyth,* or ventriloquist, who does all the talking for somebody made of wood.

quodlibetarian (kwod′li bi târ′ē ən) One who enjoys debating fine or subtle points (quodlibets) just for the mental joy or stimulation of it. Points like "What's the difference between an alien invader and an invading alien?" (Interrogative quodlibets can sometimes sound like Zen koans or lead-ins to jokes.) The original quodlibetarians did their hair-splitting thing as a form of theological or academic recreation.

sibilator (sib′ə lā′tər) The sibilant speaker, whose *s*'s are extremely wet and hissy, resulting in sentences that have the sound of an overtaxed steam radiator. Hearing a sibilator say "Sister Suzie sews sheets" is like hearing a cluster of riled snakes or undergoing a spray-can attack. Many buzzing females who like to chew gum and whisper gossip become sibilators. So do men who articulate with intense theatricality (or who are faisandé). Other sibilators may just have a loose tooth somewhere.

somniloquist (som nil′ə kwist) The sleep-talker, who still has something to say (to whom?) after climbing into bed and going unconscious. Snatches of soundtrack from a restless dozer's dreams can often be interesting, but some somniloquists can get into trouble by muttering or moaning names other than their bedmate's. Other somniloquists soliloquize merely because they've forgotten they've fallen asleep.

spintext (spin′tekst′) The longwinded, not too compelling preacher, or the priest, minister or rabbi whose sermons are a weekly ordeal. Nobody likes to be caught napping in a pew, but when a deadly, droning spintext is in the pulpit, the battle is on to keep the mind from dozing and the eyes from closing. Those long-suffering listeners are usually spoken at, not to, and rarely for by the boring homilist.

tintinnabulum (tin′ti nab′yə ləm) A "poet" who mechanically rhymes and rhymes, creating verse like the little bell on the door of a busy pawnshop. The tintinnabulum—a rhymester often found in very local newspapers—is the dogged, would-be poet, one who loves climactic echoes at the ends of lines of verse that others are sorry they ever began reading. A true clinker, literarily, but a *heliconist* (rabid versifier) whose crambo (cheap rhyming) is always appreciated in the greeting-card industry.

wit-snapper (wit′snap′ər) The quipster, ever avid to break off a snappy little remark that strikes a witty or sardonic note. Before you've finished your sentence, old wit-snapper is rounding or sharpening it off. Not to be confused with a whippersnapper, whose asides may be affronts.

xenoepist (zə nō′ə pist) A person who speaks with a foreign accent. Usually a recent stranger to the language, although some people who move to another country at a relatively early age remain xenoepists all their lives. Among other things—think of Greta Garbo or Charles Boyer—xenoepy can be very sexy.

TWENTY-ONE

HYDROPOTS, JEJUNATORS & TENTERBELLIES

EATERS, DRINKERS, AND DIETERS

Of food preferences, table manners, gourmets and gluttons

anthropophaginian (an′thrə pof′ə jin′ē ən) Or *anthropophagite*. A cannibal, or human being with the one kind of diet that will probably never become the gimmick for an American nonfiction bestseller. In some cultures anthropophaginians are born rather than made, but others sometimes emerge because of a harsh survival situation. A meal at which the entrée is human flesh is called a Thyestian banquet (after the mythological Thyestes, who unwittingly dined on his own offspring).

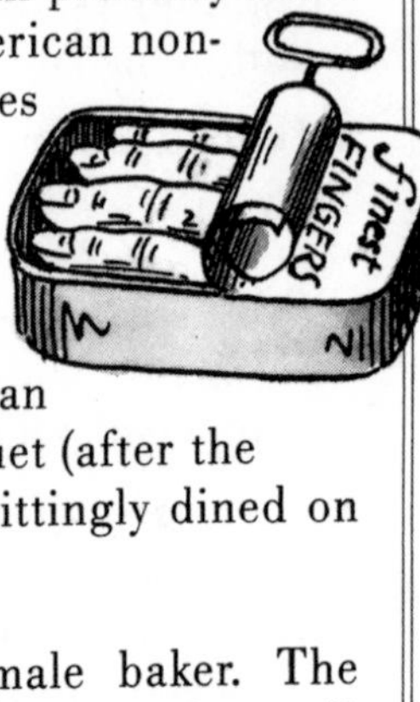

backstress (bak′stres′) A female baker. The word is related to both "baker" and "baxter," but—given all that bending over to deposit dough in the oven—why not appreciate its accidental suggestion of stress on the back?

galactophagist (gal′ak tof′ə jist) Not a monstrous devourer of galaxies but a mere, harmless milk drinker. Suckling infants are galactophagists. So are guzzling, red-blooded, white-mustached teenagers and, not by choice, older people who hate milk but have ulcers. A constant drinker of skim milk is a butterfat-less galactophagist.

helluo (hel′yōō ō′) A big, big eater, the glutton for replenishment, whose mouth always gives a big, warm welcome to anything edible. Also known as a *bellygod* or *Phaeacian.* With food, the helluo is into quantity (unlike the gourmet, who insists on quality). Nobody likes to be called a glutton (one of the seven deadly sins) or gormandizer, so why not keep in reserve this odd little borrowing from Latin?

hydropot (hī′drə pot′) A water drinker. And a pungent little word for an aqua quaffer, somebody who merely has a liking for our odorless, colorless and tasteless staple of life, H_2O. But maybe a properly emphatic word, as some hydropots are erstwhile dipsomaniacs, who choose to continue with the medium (liquid) but without the message (alcohol).

ichthyophagist (ik′thē of′ə jist) A fish eater, or somebody who may eat one if by land but always two if by sea. Confirmed ichthyophagists, or sea-loving vegetarians, have a bone to pick with *creophagists, carnivores* and *sarcophags*—the meat eaters. And might well call a butcher a *bovicide*, or bull-killer.

jejunator (jē′jə nā′tər) The person who fasts, whether for religious reasons or dietary goals. There are still many people who starve themselves periodically for a spiritual cause, but most Western jejunators just want to get that weight off with all deliberate speed.

magirist (mə jī′rist) The expert cook, or the magician in the kitchen when it comes to the baking, boiling, broiling, roasting and frying of food or the preparing of succulent cold dishes. (A regular restaurateur is a *traiteur.*) "But is she a magirist?'' mothers always want to know about a future daughter-in-law (if not in those precise words). A person who is a shameful chef, or non-magirist, becomes, like a good boxer, a take-out artist.

MYCOPHAGIST
One man's poison.

mycophagist (mī kof′ə jist) A mushroom fancier. Or a "fungus eater," although the only fungi of interest to mycophagists are the edible, rubbery, umbrella-shaped varieties.

omophagist (ō mof′ə jist) An eater of raw meat, or a person who loves steak tartare and wouldn't waste an uncooked sirloin on a black eye.

opsophagist (op sof′ə jist) The eater of excellently savory, unusually rich delicacies (though what is a delicacy to one person may be quite revolting to another). Those who dine on such epicurean dainties as snails, truffles and pheasant are usually relatively wealthy, of course. Truly rich eaters.

pantophagist (pan tof′ə jist) The come-one, come-all eater, devourer of anything and everything. The great egalitarian of eaters, the pantophagist never saw (to paraphrase Will Rogers) a dish he or she didn't like. Another word for this human garbage pail is *omnivore.*

philoxenist (fi lok′sə nist) The homebody or social cook who is most content when showing xenodochy: hospitality to strangers. Happy the stray divorcee or frozen-dinner bachelor who makes the acquaintance of a philoxenist or two. And happy the philoxenist.

poltophagist (pol tof′ə jist) The extremely thorough food chewer, determined to reduce a rock-hard carrot or bounceable piece of liver to the consistency of porridge; that is, to Fletcherize, an early 20th-century term derived from the name of a man who advocated the meticulous chewing of food. The poltophagist has determined teeth, either for the cause of better digestion or just for the joy of moving the chin around and thinking at the same time. A patient human food processor, and the counterpart to the *psomophagist.*

psomophagist (sə mof′ə jist) One of those people who bolt—or barely bother to chew—their food, whose eating style is down the hatch with solids as well as liquids (undoubtedly thereby producing gases farther on down the pike). The galloping gullet who attacks food as if he or she hasn't eaten in weeks is not regarded as a model of table manners.

tenterbelly (ten′tər bel′ē) A person with a belly distended solely from overeating, or a pig-out potbelly. (A tenter is a cloth stretcher.) Such abdominal bulldozers sometimes don't see their own shoes for years, sometimes not even their belts. Another nice old word for the feaster with the huge belly is *panguts.* Given choices, the tenterbelly always plumps for food.

trencherman (tren′chər mən) The hearty eater, or chowhound, who can really put it away and who never picks at food unless a pick and shovel are handy. One with gustatory gusto. When you say "Start right in" to the trencherman (or trencherwoman), you may be interrupting his (or her) dessert.

TWENTY-TWO

COUCH POTATOES, EPOPTS & STALKOS

HABITS, FOIBLES, AND ROLES

Preferences, eccentricities and fates

Box and Cox (boks′ ən koks′) Two people who share the same house or apartment but never see each other. Co-residents in such a curious living arrangement may work different hours, or may find each other intolerable and enjoy sharing the rent in an atmosphere of tense mutual absence. From an 1891 English farce, later popularized by Gilbert & Sullivan, about two gents who unknowingly rent the same room, one by day, one by night. Two people who alternate doing or performing the same thing are also a Box and Cox.

couch potato (kouch′ pə tā′tō) The habitual, unbudgeable television watcher, one warm and settled-in lump before the boob tube. The couch potato is never happier than when slumped down comfortably for hours before the flickering two-dimensional fires of the home screen, preferably next to a fellow couch potato or slouch tomato.

cruciverbalist (kroo͞′sə vûr′bə list) A crossword puzzle addict, one of the millions whose day is not complete until they have penciled letters into those printed grids of numbered squares. The cruciverbalist is less interested in going out and around than Down and Across. Serious cruciverbalists don't like others filling in for them.

egressor (ē gres′ər) Not a misspelled attacker but a person who goes out (unlike the *ingressor*, who comes in). Teenagers always want to go out, and quickly become resourceful egressors. Stern fathers warn daughter egressors not to be curfew transgressors with boy aggressors.

epopt (ep′opt) Anyone initiated into or instructed in a secret system, or a tyro of the cryptic. The original epopts were students of religious mysteries. In the modern world, the epopt is given a set of keys to other secret systems, from fraternity rituals to clandestine espionage procedures. One who interprets or initiates others into mysteries is a *mystagogue*.

erythrophobe (i rith′rə fōb′) This is the lady or gentleman who has a terror of blushing, and tends to be red-faced about it. Erythrophobes are the way they are probably because of being teased from a young age about looking like a fire engine when somebody tells a dirty joke.

exlex (ek′sleks′) A person (or group) acting without legal authority, literally outside the law. Usurping dictators, jewelry vendors without permits, homeowners with illegal cable TV hookups, double-parkers—exlexes all.

gongoozler (gon′ go͞o′zlər) The open-mouthed starer or the idle, curious person who tends to fall into states of prolonged, transfixed gawking. Sort of a conservative, less rubbery rubbernecker, or *gapeseed.* This is an old slang term of English canal men that applies to gongoozlers anywhere, from rural mountaintops to city sidewalks. What kind of person do they go agape at? A breathing object of wonder or curiosity, or a *gapingstock* (also called a *gapeseed*).

hypnobate (hip′nə bāt′) A sleepwalker; otherwise known as a *somnambulist, noctambulist* or *noctambule.* This sounds like a skill, and probably is (a person skilled at reclining with the eyes kept open is an insomniac). In their gaits, most nocturnal sleeping strollers either imitate the Frankenstein monster or just shuffle slowly, pandiculating (stretching their arms out stiffly) in the direction of the refrigerator. Few seem to sleepwalk in a sprint, crouch or goose step. Having two hypnobates under the same roof can be dangerous.

jehu (jē′hyo͞o′) A fast or reckless driver. Whether always in a four-wheeled hurry or turned on by the game of beating red lights, the jehu is the precipitate personality of locomotion, as pumped up as a full gas tank. Jehu was a king of Israel reputed for furious chariot attacks; later, a jehu was a coach driver who didn't spare the horses. Today's revved-up automotive speeder can also be called a *phaeton* or a *heavy foot.*

kilobytophobe (kil′ə bī′tə fōb′) The anxious computer illiterate: one of the growing number of otherwise normal folk who are quietly panicked by the realization that they know nothing about computers. The kilobytophobe gets the cold sweats around talk of PCs and analogs and longs for what "hardware" used to mean—tools and housewares in a dusty store. Combating the computer revolution is a losing battle. The refuters are down.

latitant (lat′ə tənt) Somebody in hiding, usually to escape punishment. Young Sally who hides in her backyard treehouse because she fears Mommy is going to spank her is a typical family latitant, and young Vito Corleone when he lies low is a typical Family latitant. Other latitants have purely asocial reasons for keeping a no-profile, like avoiding certain unappealing people.

lucubrator (lo͞o′kyo͝o brā′tər) The one who studies long into the night (or "composes by lamplight," as the original Latin has it), or who gives deep thought to something. You can lucubrate in the daytime also, and even in public, but the true cogitabund (deep-thinking) lucubrator is the late-night scholar. One who keeps an all-night vigil, without books, is not a lucubrator but a *pernoctalian.*

lupus in fabula (lo͞o′pəs in fab′yə lə) Or the "wolf in the tale": the person being talked about who suddenly and unexpectedly makes an appearance. Sometimes the lupus in fabula enters the room just in time to hear the tail end of a compliment. More often, his or her unexpected arrival brings all conversation to an awkward, deafening halt. Speak of the devil.

melomaniac (mel′ō mā′nē ak′) The total music addict, Mr. or Ms. Superlistener. If ever there was an Age of Melomania, it is now, when half the population is jogging, typing, commuting, studying or just hanging out with music literally plugged into the ears. Music going in the background all the time? The melomaniac of the '80s—the headset humanoid—has it going in the cranial foreground, ear to ear. A lover of harsh sounds is a *cacophonophilist.*

mossback (môs′bak′) A duffer or gaffer (female duffer), or even somebody, not that old, who is very old-fashioned or downright reactionary. (A mossback is also a rustic or backwoods type, but some moss has grown over that meaning.) Either behind the times or plain against them, the mossback respects the old, tried-and-true values and

MELOMANIAC
Always tuned in.

ways. Also known as a *moldy fig* (which more specifically means someone who prefers Dixieland to modern jazz).

nicotian (ni kō′shən) Not a misspelling, and an obvious meaning: a user of tobacco. This includes the individual who is fumiferous, or smoke-producing, or who leaves a frowst (stale or musty odor) in a room with his or her mundungus (offensive tobacco); the more folksy user of chewing tobacco, who doesn't need matches but does a lot of spitting; and the snuff dipper.

PACK-RAT
Why throw anything away?

pack-rat (pak′rat′) The uncontrollable collector—with a compulsion to hold on to possessions, however useless, old or cluttering they are. Instead of hoarding wealth, this able-retentive hoards junk, for the most part, and throws nothing out except his or her back (from all that lifting and stacking). The organizational newsletter of the pack-rats is "The Irrational Acquirer."

peckerwood (pek′ər wŏŏd′) A poor white person of the rural Southern variety. A backwoods type. (The word is a backward version of "woodpecker.") You may not live in the South, but you see peckerwoods depicted in those trashy white-trash movies about country singers, redneck sheriffs, moonshine stills and 30-vehicle pileups.

polyposist (pol′ē pō′sist) A hard drinker; the major boozehound who when nosing into the alcohol doesn't take prisoners or count rounds. No cocktail sipper, this is the lush, the serial quaffer who knocks it back, slug by slug. Excessive hard drinkers, or crapulous polyposists, sometimes become *hydropots* or *nephalists.*

querent (kwir′ənt) One who consults an astrologer (or, presumably, carefully checks daily horoscopes in the newspaper), as opposed to one who consults a *scryer,* or crystal gazer. If you're not yourself a querent, you doubtless know quite a few—people ever receptive to tips on today and tomorrow according to the current shenanigans of the stars and planets. Querents speak in Sign language, from Aquarius to Capricorn.

roturier (rō tŏŏr′ē ā′) A *parvenu* or *nouveau riche,* or a plebeian who has made some money: well off but a bit obvious or ostentatious about it because of a certain lack of class. The word originally referred to a non-noble landholder. Another old word for a richie of humble origins is *ruptuary.*

sedens (sē′denz) The dweller (or *commorant*) who stays and lives in the area where he or she was born; a stay-around-home rather than a stay-at-home. At high school reunions, moved-away graduates always encounter a number of sedentes (as the plural goes): classmates who hung around the old hometown, who are still, surprisingly, locals. A native, anywhere, is an *autochthon* or *indigene* and a colonizer is an *oecist.*

shunpiker (shun′pī′kər) The driver who avoids highways for byways, taking slower but more relaxing and scenic back roads instead. The shunpiker cares about more than just getting there and rules out the big red route lines on maps, the major-hassle arteries. Give him or her the calmer minor thoroughfare, the country air, the pleasure of tooling along on the old blacktop.

silentiary (sī len′chē er′ē) One privy to state secrets, as a diplomat, government worker or spy, and under oath not to divulge them; a true member of the silent service. Silentiaries are always tiptoeing about, as in this security-clearance age of big government, semi-cold war, high-tech secrets and full-scale espionage. As are lapsed silentiaries—otherwise known as defectors or traitors. The word can also denote both an official whose job is to keep order in court and a person observing silence for religious reasons.

stalko (stô′kō) The impecunious, down-and-out vagrant posing as a gentleman, complete with stiff bow, stiff dignity and maybe stiff alcohol content as well; the chap who's déclassé but prefers to act distingué. An Anglo-Irish word for one of the endurable characters in human society and comedy: the bum who puts on airs.

surbater (sûr′bā′tər) That person with dogged dogs—who walks too fast for anybody's liking. (To surbate is to wear out the feet.) A born plodder should avoid the company of a surbater unless it involves stationary positions, or unless he or she is allowed a head start or contractual rest stops. Some surbaters are hale, long-striding hikers. Some are latent marathoners or race-walkers. And some are just spry little old ladies in jogging shoes. One averse to walking at all is a *basiphobe.*

triskaidekaphobe (tris′kī dek′ə fōb′) Or *tridecaphobe.* A person superstitious about the number 13. This applies to numbers bet on, number of guests invited, those infamous Fridays, and sports uniforms. Fortunately, there are only 12 zodiac signs (think what astrologers would make of the omens of a 13th sign) and no sports with 13 on a team side. For some reason, nobody seems to want to skip his or her thirteenth birthday.

Ucalegon (yo͞o kal′ə gon′) A Ucalegon is a neighbor whose house is on fire. It seems impossible that there should be a word for this, but here you are (courtesy of Trojan legend, in which Ucalegon was an unfortunate, burned-out neighbor of Aeneas). An extremely rare word, though one should not be burning to have a chance to use it. A mere neighbor, whose house may or may not be in flames, is an *accolent.*

CANOODLER
Master of the touch system.

TWENTY-THREE

CANOODLERS, RENIFLEURS & VIRVESTITES

SEX

The desirable, the undesirable, the kinky

aberrant (a ber′ənt) Your everyday human being with a strange, closeted personal practice or habit, some bit of behavior or misbehavior not exactly to be demonstrated to others. We're talking sex here, what else? The aberrant is your average deviate. The one with kinks, who doesn't necessarily want to iron them out.

algolagnist (al′gō lag′nist) One whose biggest sexual thrill is pain, either his or her own or that bestowed on somebody else. In short, either a masochist or a sadist, and maybe both. Gentleness and a sensitive touch are not favorite styles of foreplay here.

barber's chair (bär′bərz châr′) The come-one, come-all prostitute or town whore, or a woman who brassily strumpets her sexual availability to all local, action-seeking males. Otherwise known as a tasteless tart, under-the-bridge trull, or tramp steaming. A reformed prostitute is a *convertite* or a *Magdalene.*

canoodler (kə nōō′dlər) The amorous caresser, or the lover expressing his or her fondle for the object of affection. Nothing too heavy, mind you. Canoodling is just some healthy messing around:

nuzzling, hugging, squeezing or making sure the bodily contours are still there, as opposed to more urgent exploration. Canoodlers press the flesh in a making-out way. They must be careful not to get into contrectation, an improbable but actual word for foreplay or heavy petting.

celadon (sel′ə don′) The proverbial wan lover, weak from ardor, pallid from passion. One hears often of women languishing. The celadon is a boy or man who is languishing.

chicken hawk (chik′ən hôk′) A man who preys on teenage boys to satisfy his homosexual needs. (There doesn't seem to be a term with real claws for a male who preys on teenage girls.)

cisvestite (sis ves′tīt) Unlike the *berdache* (transvestite), the cisvestite wears same-sex clothing. But the clothing is inappropriate or even weird, and in most cases represents an attempt to look younger—see the blue-haired matron in the pinafore or the graying male "swinger" in designer jeans. And, too, trying to look older, the young girl in purple lipstick and Mom's high heels.

crotch-watcher (kroch′woch′ər) The woman whose eye is always taking note of men's crotches, their degree of bulge, as a way of checking out the possible or impossible contents; a male equipment estimator: Is he or is he not mentulate, or well hung? (This goes to show that when a maiden lowers her eyes, it isn't always out of modesty.) A female fly-by-day critic. The male homosexual who is interested in men's inseams is a *basketeer* or *basket-watcher.*

ecdysiast (ek diz′ē əst) A stripteaser, or indulger in titillating anacalypsis (or regaling unveiling).

We owe this word to H. L. Mencken, who invented it at the request of famous stripper Georgia Sothern. It used to be only women who made a performance out of fluffing their fans at their best lines, but today we have male strippers keeping spectators up on what's coming off.

écouteur (ek′o͞o to͝or′) The erotic eavesdropper, the aural equivalent of the voyeur; he or she who gets sexually aroused by overhearing the hot activities of neighboring others—the couple coupling noisily next door, say, or the rhythmic ceiling drumming not of an upstairs musician but of an upstairs bed.

exosculator (ek sos′kyə lā′tər) Not just a kisser but a hearty, fond kisser. Those big, wet smackers by your loving Aunt Hilda? That boy who used to engulf your ear with his mouth and wet it with his cervisial (beery) tongue? A kiss is not just a kiss when delivered by an avid exosculator.

frotteur (frô to͝or′) That frontally restless male (an advanced cousin to the less forceful flasher) who likes to rub up against female bodies, especially female buttocks, in crowded public places. The act itself is called frottage, and the victim usually takes a few moments to realize what she is up against—that the friction is not fiction. Frotteurs, it is important to note, rub up against the law the wrong way.

genicon (jen′ə kən) That fantasied sexual partner, as opposed to the one you're actually stuck with. The fantasy lover who wants to do everything, who lets you do anything. Or who looks like—what was his name? Do one's genicons change over the years? Over the nights? Genicons

GENOPHOBE
Nervous about the facts of life.

can appear in dreams, too, and a female one who is more than a male sleeper can bear is an oneirogmos, or wet dream.

genophobe (jen′ə fōb′) The male or female who is very uneasy about anything having to do with sex—an otherwise normal adult who remains uptight about down there. Genophobes have been informed about the birds and the bees, but they don't like (or aren't cocksure about) what they've heard and tend to go catatonic when beyond the platonic.

gynotikolobomassophile (gī not′ə kō lō′-bō mas′ə fīl′) The fond nuzzler and nibbler of women's earlobes. Especially on a female, the earlobe is considered an authorized erogenous zone (and all males know that whispering sweet nothings above the lobes can initiate good aural sex). A word unearthed for us by Josefa Heifetz Byrne and included in her own remarkable dictionary. The gynotikolobomassophile, whispering or not, is a true necker.

melcryptovestimentaphile (mel kript′ō-vest′ə men′tə fīl′) The male who has a healthy or unhealthy attraction to women's black underwear. For the serious melcryptovestimentaphile, black lacy fripperies and frills and furbelows on a woman's body make for lingerie that lingers in the mind. And if a lady enjoys wearing dark and devilish undies, she's a melcryptovestimentaphile, too. A humorous coinage brought to our attention by author and lexical cornucopia Willard Espy.

POSSLQ (pos′əl kyo͞o′) For "Person of Opposite Sex Sharing Living Quarters." Heterosexually speaking, one's significant other or, in most cases, live-in lover in lieu of a legal spouse. Who would expect that an exotic creature called a "posselcue" (as it is pronounced) would be created—coined—by the bureaucracy of the U.S. government?

renifleur (ren′ə flo͝or′) A sly or sleazy sniffer, sexually aroused by people's body odors or even the aroma of urine. Not your neighbor's dog, but the active human scenter, the randy renifleur, with a constant nose for the gamy or the funky.

retifist (ret′ə fist) The shoe fetishist, aroused by admiring, touching, sniffing, or somehow having foreplay or sex with an irresistible piece of footwear. As retifists are mostly heterosexual males, footwear usually means high heels, pumps, slingbacks, mules, or Lady Adidas sneaks with pompom socks. What retifists really like is feet, of course, but these are harder to molest or collect. The psychology books tell us that the term comes from the name of an 18th-century French educator, Rétif (or Restif) de la Bretonne. Educator?

spintry (spin′trē) A homosexual male prostitute, or a young man who takes up the slack of the flesh trade not handled by the old (and oldest) firm of Trollop, Trull, Harlot & Strumpet. A rare word, but with the hundreds of pungent words that exist (or did) for the female hustler, it seems only right to resurrect at least one interesting one (from a Latin word) for the "gentleman of the night."

subvirate (sub′və rāt′) A man whose virility is subnormal—or "whose manhood is imperfect," as one dictionary puts it. That is, the clearly unmasculine male, who may never even get to the stage of performance anxiety because he has total rehearsal apathy. Strangely undersexed men often prefer TV sitcoms, computer books, sleep, cookies or toy soldiers to the company of a redblooded woman. A subvirate with an equipment problem may be a *spado.*

tribade (trib′əd) A lesbian, or *sapphist.* An exotic term from older times and musty sexology books that means, in the original Greek, "she who rubs" (against another she).

troilist (troi′list) The sexual participant who gets lonely with only one partner and prefers two at the same time. The troilist is one-third of the celebrated ménage à trois. The adjustment of limbs in these complicated carnal get-togethers can get tricky, and some troilists merely want the third party to watch, not to party.

virvestite (vir ves′tīt) A girl or woman who prefers wearing male clothing—or who does not want to lose her viraginity (maleness). What constitutes male clothing today may be debatable, but the virvestite is always happier in slacks, an Oxford button-down and a rumpled sweatshirt than in a dress and nylons. A female radically into menswear may go for the necktie, workboots and athletic supporter. To keep up with male fashions nowadays, the really bold and fearless virvestite will go as far as bikini briefs and the single earring.

TWENTY-FOUR

MUMPSIMUSES, PARVANIMITIES & SOLITUDINARIANS

VERY INDIVIDUAL PEOPLE

The asocial, the solitary, the strange

acephalist (ā sef′ə list) The balky maverick who acknowledges no head or superior or authority; the complete, all-the-way insubordinate. Acephalists have trouble getting hired, or staying that way. The only authority figure they look for is an effigy of the boss to burn.

aphephobe (af′ə fōb′) The person who doesn't like being touched, who's always beating a tactile retreat from a mere handshake or pat on the back (to say nothing of a hand on the knee). Aphephobes (also, *haphephobes* or *haptephobes*) have their reasons, presumably, for being physically standoffish and backoffish. Or possibly they're just a little bit, well, touched.

drapetomaniac (drap′i tə mā′nē ak′) One with an uncontrollable tendency to roam about aimlessly; a sort of daffy wanderer. The trouble with drapetomaniacs is that they usually have to be retrieved. Some start young, waddling or toddling off from Mommy at the shopping mall. But most are elderly folk stepping out into senility: Aunt Adelaide backpacking along the waterfront or Uncle Joe peregrinating to the toy store by way of the ladies' room. A solitary wanderer—who is circumforaneous, or goes from place to place—can also be called a *solivagant.*

heteroclite (het'ər ə klīt') One who goes against the accepted rules, conventions, forms, etc. You know those people who always go by the book? The heteroclite, or against-the-grainer, always goes not by the book. So heteroclites are not only rebellious or innovative but also unpredictable and even unmanageable.

isolato (ī'sə lā'tō) The philosophical or existential outcast; one who feels fundamentally estranged from the times or society he or she is stuck in. A romantic in a cynical society, a 20th-century punker in a 19th-century New England town, an intelligent woman in a redneck backwater—these are only some of the many types of isolatos in today's world. A social or societal outsider is also an *Ishmael.*

mumpsimus (mump'sə məs) The mumpsimus is quite wrong about something but, being pigheaded as well as wrong, will be damned before anybody changes his or her ways. Whether a stubborn fool or cocksure bigot, this one has gotten hold of a wacky notion and won't let go. The word comes from a pronunciation error in the Latin Mass (correctly, "sumpsimus") that a priest refused to be corrected on. The error persisted in is also called a mumpsimus, and a stickler for correctness, or a *precisian* or *punctilionist,* is correspondingly known as a *sumpsimus.*

omphalopsychite (om'fə lō sī'kīt) A navel-starer—at one's own, that is, not the belly dancer's—or one of those cross-legged mystical or

OMPHALOPSYCHITE
A studious member of the navel academy.

meditative types. Calling an Eastern head this (which sounds more like a term for an elephant doctor) should break him or her out of that trance. Spiritual navel-gazing is omphaloskepsis.

parvanimity (pär′və nim′ə tē) A petty or mean person endowed with great smallness of mind—in a sense that has nothing to do with brain diameter. This is the individual devoid of wisdom, imagination, consideration. And, of course, of broadmindedness. The word also means said smallness of mind, so that a parvanimity possesses parvanimity (not magnanimity).

rara avis (râr′ə ā′vis) An extremely, interestingly rare person, one who doesn't fit any mold. A "rare bird," literally, and generally an estimable one, as opposed to a queer duck.

skell (skel) A grungy derelict, or street person of the round-the-clock rather than pedestrian variety. The skell can be identified by garb in the styling of oily dropcloths and Emmett Kelly, but also by a certain air of comfort when seated on a curb between a mountain of refuse-filled green Baggies and a fire hydrant. Mentally, skells tend to be eccentric or a little around the bend.

solitudinarian (sol′ə to͞o′də nâr′ē ən) The loner who prizes the solitary life, who wants to be alone, thank you. Meeting too many of the wrong people in life can be conducive to being reclusive. But some solitudinarians have been soloists since birth, which was possibly when it first, immediately, occurred to them that they preferred to be alone.

suist (so͞o′ist) The person whose philosophy is simple: suit yourself, follow your own inclinations. The suist makes decisions according to personal beliefs or desires, unfazed by approval or disapproval from others. Understandably, suists (also known as *thelemites*) are often pleasure seekers and libertines.

PRONUNCIATION KEY

c**a**t	t**oi**l	**ch**ip
d**ā**te	c**o͞o**l	**g**ive
c**ä**lm	t**o͝o**k	**j**oy
f**â**re	**ou**t	**k**eep
l**e**nd	sh**u**t	si**ng**
ēve	t**û**rn	**sh**ow
p**i**t	ə { **a**long	**th**in
m**ī**ce	tight**e**n	**y**ou
c**o**p	poss**i**ble	**zh**:
v**ō**te	lem**o**n	mea**s**ure
f**ô**rd	foc**u**s	

A bold prime mark (**′**) after a syllable indicates a primary or strong stress; a lighter mark (′) indicates a secondary or lighter stress. Alternative pronunciations are not given, although many exist. Pronunciations of non-English terms are approximate.

INDEX

D

E

F

N

O

P

Q

R

S